VGM Careers for You Series

W9-CJE-195

CAREERS
F O R
HISTORY
BUFFS
& Others Who
Learn From The Past

Blythe Camenson

VGM Career Horizons
a division of *NTC Publishing Group*
Lincolnwood, Illinois USA

Library of Congress Cataloging-in-Publication Data is available from the Library of Congress

Published by VGM Career Horizons, a division of NTC Publishing Group
4255 West Touhy Avenue
Lincolnwood (Chicago), Illinois 60646-1975, U.S.A.
© 1994 by NTC Publishing Group. All rights reserved.
No part of this book may be reproduced, stored in a retrieval system, or transmitted in any form or by any means, electronic, mechanical, photocopying, recording or otherwise, without the prior permission of NTC Publishing Group.
Manufactured in the United States of America.

5 6 7 8 9 0 VP 9 8 7 6 5 4 3 2

Dedication

T o all the people who came before us, for without them we would have no history, and no avid interest to consume us.

Contents

About the Author

G rowing up in historic New England, it's easy to see how Blythe Camenson became an avid history buff. Surrounded by red brick and ivy, Victorian gingerbread, and quaint and picturesque seaports and harbors, the love of history became second nature to her. Through her travels overseas in Europe and the Middle East, her interests broadened.

Camenson works as a free-lance writer specializing in career and travel. She has written numerous articles for magazines and newspapers and, after spending eight years in the Middle East, she wrote the book, *Working in the Persian Gulf—Survival Secrets for Men and Women (The Real Story)* (Desert Diamond Books, 1991). She also conducts and organizes workshops and seminars for writers.

The author has extensive teaching and counseling experience, most of it accumulated in the Middle East. She has taught English as a foreign language to university students in Riyadh and at Sultan Qaboos University in Muscat, Oman. Camenson also worked as an educational counselor to Middle Eastern students, both in Kuwait and Washington, D.C. Her last posting overseas, as director of courses at the American Cultural Center in Baghdad, Iraq, ended after the Iraqi invasion of Kuwait. Nine days after the invasion, Camenson was included in the first convoy from the U.S. embassy to be evacuated overland to the Jordanian border.

Camenson earned her Bachelor of Arts degree, with a double major in English and psychology, from the University of Massachusetts, Boston, in 1973. In 1976 she received her Master's of Education (M.Ed.) degree in counseling from Northeastern University, also in Boston.

A Word from the Author

While interviewing the thirty or so professionals for this book, I was struck again and again by the one thing all these diverse people had in common. From tour guides working for an hourly wage to chiefs and directors at the top of the salary scale, all of them, unequivocally, expressed their love for the work they are doing.

I think it is rare to find so many people satisfied with their professions, and I think it says something unique and wonderful about the field of history.

For those of you reading this book for help in selecting a career, or deciding upon a career change, I feel I can safely tell you that no matter what aspect of the field you choose to follow, you will find yourself employed in a stimulating environment with dedicated and congenial coworkers.

You probably won't become famous, and you definitely won't get rich, but I do believe you will be happy.

Who can ask for anything more?

—Blythe Camenson

Acknowledgments

T he author would like to thank the following history lovers for providing information about their careers:

Don Albro   Director of Historic Sites
               Joseph Smith Historic Center
               Nauvoo, Illinois

Patricia Baker   Wardrobe and Textiles Manager
               Plimoth Plantation
               Plymouth, Massachusetts

Peter Benton   Restoration Architect
               John Milner and Associates, Inc.
               West Chester, Pennsylvania

Jeff Donnelly   Volunteer Tour Guide
               Miami Design Preservation League
               Miami Beach, Florida

Tom Doyle   Carriage Tour Operator
               Palmetto Carriage Works, Ltd.
               Charleston, South Carolina

John Fleckner   Chief Archivist
                         National Museum of American
                            History, Smithsonian Institution
                         Washington, D.C.

Mark Fortenberry   Curator of Structures
                         Nantucket Historical Association
                         Nantucket, Massachusetts

Jeremy Fried   Character Interpreter
                         Colonial Williamsburg Foundation
                         Williamsburg, Virginia

Tom Gerhardt   Interpretive Artisan: Cooper
                         Plimoth Plantation
                         Plymouth, Massachusetts

Hank Grasso   Exhibit Designer
                         National Museum of American
                            History, Smithsonian Institution
                         Washington, D.C.

Kristin Kuckelman   Field Archeologist
                         Crow Canyon Archaelological Center
                         Cortez, Colorado

Kendra Lambert   Former Student Intern
                         National Museum of American
                            History, Smithsonian Institution
                         Washington, D.C.

Michael Larsen   Literary Agent/Author
                         San Francisco, California

Antoinette Lee   Historian
                         National Register of Historic Places
                         Washington, D.C.

Carol Levin	Vintage Clothing Specialist Stock Exchange Wilton Manors, Florida
Deb Mason	Pottery Supervisor, Crafts Center Plimoth Plantation Plymouth, Massachusetts
Charles McGovern	Curator National Museum of American History, Smithsonian Institution Washington, D.C.
George Neary	Administrative Director/Information Officer Miami Design Preservation League Miami Beach, Florida
Cookie O'Brien	Columnist Historic St. Augustine Preservation Board St. Augustine, Florida
Adam Perl	Antique Dealer Pastimes Ithaca, New York
Elizabeth Pomada	Literary Agent/Author San Francisco, California
Joel Pontz	Supervisor of Interpretive Artisans Plimoth Plantation Plymouth, Massachusetts
Mary Ptak	Vintage Clothing Specialist Stock Exchange Wilton Manors, Florida

Jim Ridolfi   Auctioneer
                             Aspon Trading Company
                             Troy, Pennsylvania

Roger and Mary   Proprietors
Schmidt   18 Gardner Street Inn
                             Nantucket, Massachusetts

Jeremy Slavitz   Docent
                             Nantucket Historical Association
                             Nantucket, Massachusetts

Prudy Taylor Board   Publisher
                             Prudy's Press
                             Fort Myers, Florida

Carolyn Travers   Director of Research
                             Plimoth Plantation
                             Plymouth, Massachusetts

Gordie Wilson   Superintendent
                             Castillo de San Marcos National
                                Monument
                             St. Augustine, Florida

CHAPTER ONE

Jobs for History Buffs

A lthough the United States might be considered a young country, at least by the rest of the world's standards, it is still a land steeped in history. Throughout the country there are thousands of historic houses and public buildings, restored or reconstructed villages—even entire cities—to explore.

And always the melting pot, America is ripe with relics of past visitors and civilizations—Vikings, early Native American culture, Spanish and French settlements, Pilgrims, Colonialists, and forgers of the Wild West, to name just a few.

Many history buffs don't limit their interests to America. There's a whole world out there—Europe and Asia, Africa and South America, even Australia—with millennia of cultures and events to examine.

What Makes a History Buff?

History buffs are fascinated by events, places, and people from the past. There are armchair historians, devouring innumerable biographies and researched accounts, as well as hands-on types, out in the field digging for artifacts, exploring the lanes and roadways our ancestors once walked, or fighting to preserve historic buildings and monuments.

History buffs possess qualities as diverse as the areas of interests to explore. Some are thrilled by the discovery of research or are collectors and catalogers by nature. They might enjoy working with their hands, recreating early American crafts with a potter's wheel or hand plane, or duplicating period clothing. To some, preserving and restoring the lines and structures of historic houses and buildings hold great interest.

Others love the smell of old books and paper and spend most of their time in libraries or government or private archives. Still others enjoy sharing their knowledge through talks and presentations or through the written word. They've found their niche working with the public as tour guides or information officers or writing articles and booklets for publication.

The traits history buffs do have in common are their insatiable curiosity and their love of the relics, events, people, and places of the past.

The Employment Outlook

Public interest in preserving our American heritage has grown tremendously in recent years. Where once settings in which history buffs could find employment were limited to a few museums and libraries, there are now thousands of new opportunities across the country. Every state has several departments devoted to different aspects of its local history. Most major cities, and even small towns, support a variety of historical societies and preservation boards. More and more historic buildings are nominated each year for inclusion on the National Register; many of these sites are operated as historic house museums open to the public.

New job titles have been added to the list once limited to curators and librarians. The field of history is now open to all sorts of professionals, including restoration specialists, designers, planners, financiers, audience advocates, information specialists, and many more.

Although the competition in some sectors is stiff, and funding always seems to lag behind public demand, a persistent history buff can get his or her foot in the door through volunteering or participating in a student internship.

Heaven-sent Jobs for History Buffs

Job-hunting history buffs dream of finding a position where their skills and interests can be combined. Would any of these help wanted ads send you racing to the post office to mail off your resume?

RESEARCHER Author seeks experienced researcher for project documenting restored Victorian houses. Must be willing to travel.

TOUR GUIDE Outgoing person with good communication skills needed to guide special interest groups through American history museum in Washington, D.C.

POTTER Fine-arts major familiar with or willing to learn seventeenth-century crafts techniques for demonstrating at living history museum.

DIG SITE ASSISTANT Position open for energetic student or recent graduate at major archeological dig site in New Mexico. Duties include cleaning and recording discovered artifacts.

INFORMATION OFFICER Historic site preservation board has opening for officer to disseminate information to the public. Good writing skills necessary. Bilingual, Spanish/English a plus.

Qualifications

Required qualifications vary depending on the job. Although many employers prefer their applicants to have a bachelor's or higher degree in history or a related field, not all do. Theater majors make excellent tour guides and character interpreters. Parks and recreation majors are a shoo-in with the National Park Service.

Many jobs discussed in this book don't require a college degree at all. In some situations the following qualifications are more important: experience, extensive knowledge of a particular time period or region, the ability to communicate with diverse groups of people, good writing skills and research skills.

Salaries

Salaries vary widely from position to position but are generally low, as are most pay scales for education-related fields. Factors such as the source of funding or the region of the country determine salary levels more so than the complexity of the job or the level of the candidates' education and experience.

Some jobs pay only hourly wages, others follow the federal government's GS scale. A tour guide might earn $6 to $10 an hour, an information officer perhaps $25,000 to $30,000 a year, a restoration architect in the $30,000 to $40,000 range annually.

Most jobs provide benefits such as health insurance. But all those interviewed on the pages to come stressed that financial rewards were not the main reason, or even a consideration, in pursuing their chosen professions. The low pay is far outweighed by the satisfaction of doing work they love.

Choosing a Profession

With so many areas of history to explore, how do you know which avenue would be right for you? Take a look at the chart that follows. Find your interests and skills, then look across to identify career options. You'll see that many of the job titles combine more than one interest. A short description of some of these jobs follows the chart; more in-depth discussions will be found in the chapters to come.

INTERESTS AND SKILLS	JOB TITLES
OLD HOUSES	Restoration Architect, Architectural Historian, Curator of Structures, Preservationist, Curator, Exhibit Designer, Historic Interiors Specialist
WORKING WITH YOUR HANDS	Restoration Architect, Curator of Structures, Archeologist, Artisan, Archivist, Costumer, Antique Dealer, Refinisher, Exhibit Designer
FINDING OUT INFORMATION	Historian, Researcher, Archeologist, Archivist, Genealogist, Curator
WORKING WITH THE PUBLIC	Character Interpreter, Tour Guide, Information Officer, Park Ranger, Historic Inn Operator, Public Relations, Educator, Auctioneer
WRITING	Information Officer, Public Relations Representative, Curator, Archeologist
WORKING OUTDOORS	Archeologist, Restoration Architect, Character Interpreter, Curator of Structures, Park Ranger, Auctioneer

Job categories are as varied as the locations. The following paragraphs give a brief overview of the dozens of jobs discussed in this book.

Jobs for Historians

The term *historian* covers a large range of career options and job settings. In general, historians study, assess, and interpret the past to determine what happened and why. They examine court documents, diaries, letters, and newspaper accounts; they interview individuals and study archeological and artifactual evidence. They conduct research, write, teach, evaluate, and make recommendations.

Historians work in schools and universities, in libraries and museums, in government offices and private enterprises.

Jobs in Living History Museums

Do you have a good memory (and good vision)? Do you like to pore through old documents researching lives of America's ancestors? How about a flair for improvisation and the dramatic? Can you think fast on your feet? Or work with your hands? These qualities, and more, could land you a job as a researcher, character interpreter or craftworker at Colonial Williamsburg or Plimoth Plantation, two of the many living history museums throughout the country.

Jobs with the National Park Service

Most people picture a park ranger for the National Park Service dressed in a snappy uniform, battling blazing forest fires with his trusty companion, Smokey the Bear, by his side. And while many rangers are concerned with fire prevention, nature and conservation, there is another category of ranger that would be of interest to history buffs. Interpretation park rangers, both men and women, work at the more than two hundred historic sites and national monuments throughout the country. This division of rangers is devoted to preserving and explaining the past.

Jobs in History Museums

History museums offer a wide range of positions, from directors and curators to educators and designers. Depending upon the position, responsibilities could include collecting, preserving, restoring, displaying, explaining, and guarding.

Jobs in Architectural History and Restoration

Lovers of the architectural styles and structures of the past are moved to study them, restore and renovate, reproduce, or preserve and protect them. They often work with their hands creating drawings or lifting beams and sanding wood trim.

Jobs with Preservation Boards and Historical Societies

People who work on preservation boards and in historical societies enjoy teamwork, serving on committees, and educating the public—and they are not afraid to fight for a cause they believe in. Through the work of dedicated preservationists across the country, thousands of historic buildings, even entire districts, have been saved from the wrecking ball. Many of these sites have gone on to achieve national recognition.

Jobs in Archeology

Do you dream of traveling—to Egypt or Israel, to Peru or Istanbul? Can you pay attention to detail and perform delicate, painstaking tasks? As an archeologist or assistant, your work could take you around the world, literally uncovering the past one grain of sand at a time.

Jobs in Genealogy

Genealogists act as detectives to the past, tracing missing persons, filling in the holes in family histories. They interview older family members; visit courthouses, cemeteries, and libraries; and spend hours poring through diaries, old newspaper accounts, marriage licenses, and birth and death certificates.

Jobs for Writers and Photographers

If you have a talent for writing, or know how to handle a camera, you can make your own presentation, sharing through words and pictures various events, places, and artifacts of historical interest. Writers and photographers produce books and pamphlets, post-cards and posters.

The Self-Employed History Buff

Want to be your own boss? There are many businesses and sidelines into which a history buff can venture, including the following examples: running an historic inn; dealing in antiques; creating, promoting, and operating your own tour company; restoring and selling vintage clothing. The list is limited only by your imagination.

The Job Hunt

Although many history buffs can find employment in their own hometown—in a local historical society or historic house museum—chances are you'll have to relocate to broaden your opportunities. If you have a spot in mind where you'd like to work, a phone call or an introductory letter sent with your resume is a good way to start. If you would like some more ideas on possible locations, there are several directories listed in the coming chapters and in the appendix which can lead you to interesting destinations.

Since many sites are state or federally operated, you might have to obtain a special application through the state capital or from Washington, D.C.

Some private employers, however, such as the Colonial Williamsburg Foundation, expect job hopefuls to apply in person. They regularly post openings and operate a job hotline with recorded messages.

Many historical organizations and professional associations produce monthly or quarterly newsletters with job listings and upcoming internships and fellowships. Some key addresses and telephone numbers, as well as suggested further readings, have been provided for you throughout the following chapters and in the appendixes.

CHAPTER TWO

Living History Museums

History Comes Alive

A living history museum is a vibrant, active village, town or city where the day-to-day life of a particular time period has been authentically recreated. Once you step through the gates, you leave the present behind. The houses and public buildings are restored originals or thoroughly researched reproductions. Interiors are outfitted with period furniture, cookware, bed linens and tablecloths. Peek under a bed and you might even find a 200- or 300-year-old mousetrap.

Residents wear the clothing of their day and discuss their dreams and concerns with visitors as they go about their daily tasks. If you were to stop a costumed gentleman passing by and ask where the nearest McDonald's is, he wouldn't seem to have any idea what you were talking about—unless he thought to direct you to a neighbor's farm. He might even do so using the dialect of his home country.

Colonial Williamsburg in Virginia and Plimoth Plantation in Massachusetts are just two examples of living history museums. Several others with addresses and telephone numbers can be found in Appendix A.

These large enterprises offer employment for professional and entry-level workers in a wide variety of categories.

These include, but are not limited to, character interpreters, presenters, costumers, and researchers.

Many sites are state or federally funded, and still more receive their support through admission tickets and private donations.

Falling into this latter category is Williamsburg, a painstakingly restored colonial-era village.

Close-up: Colonial Williamsburg

Visitors to Colonial Williamsburg meet historical figures, witness events, and participate in the daily lives of the people who helped bring about American independence.

For 81 years, from 1699 to 1780 (though only die-hard history buffs need remember the dates), Williamsburg was the thriving capital of Virginia, one of the original 13 American colonies. After the American Revolution, when the capital was moved to Richmond, Williamsburg began a decline that lasted 146 years. It became a sleepy southern town with crumbling roads and buildings, overgrown gardens, and only a distant memory of patriots and prosperity.

In 1926, with his love of American history and a belief that anything is possible, John D. Rockefeller, Jr., began the Colonial Williamsburg restoration project to return this once-important city to its former glory.

Now, after over 60 years of work, 88 original eighteenth-century and early nineteenth-century structures have been completely restored and over 500 others have been reconstructed on original foundations—but only after extensive archeological and historical investigation.

The principal thoroughfare in Williamsburg is the Duke of Gloucester Street, which began as nothing more than a winding horsepath flanked by a tavern and a few shops and houses. Then, in 1693, with the establishment of the College of William and Mary (America's second oldest university, Harvard being the first) at the western end and the impressive Capitol building at the far eastern end, the street was widened and became the busy center of daily activity. Today it is closed to traffic, though an occasional horse-drawn carriage or stage wagon clatters by. Eighteenth-century shops and houses still stand, shaded by beautiful old trees lining the hard-packed dirt walkways.

These buildings are not just empty symbols of a bygone era, however. Many of the homes shelter permanent residents—employees of the Colonial Williamsburg Foundation—or act as inns to house the many visitors who come every year.

Those that are open to the public are filled with the same artifacts, activities, and people that made up daily life in colonial times.

Character Interpreter

The most visible living history museum employees are the scores of men and women decked out in authentic period costumes. They can be found waiting inside the buildings or walking through the grounds, and although they might seem to be there just for decoration—or "photo opportunities," as they are sometimes called—most are trained researchers, actors, and presenters. A select group of these staff members use "first-person" interpretation or role playing to explain about their place in history. They are called character interpreters or people of the past. They are in actuality skilled social historians who have researched early residents and assumed their roles.

In Williamsburg, you can follow Mrs. Powell about town as this eighteenth-century housewife does her errands, or visit the Powell House and speak with Mr. Powell, the prominent Williamsburg builder.

You can spend the afternoon in the Capitol yard listening to colonial gentlemen discussing events of the day or converse with Mr. Samuel Henley, an eighteenth-century professor at the College of William and Mary, and learn about the values and traditions of his time. You can even eavesdrop on young gentlemen as they prepare for college and share their expectations and concerns for the future.

Children can join a costumed interpreter to explore the inter-action of colonial family life, youth apprenticeships, education, work, and leisure time.

Adam Waterford, a free black cooper, and young Charles, the son of the Powell family's cook, are also on hand for a glimpse into the colonial African-American experience.

At Plimoth Plantation you can listen to seventeenth-century Goodwife Cook plan her day or share tidbits of gossip with Governor Bradford's sister-in-law. John Alden is there, mak-ing barrels in his one-room cottage or helping other villagers erect a new house. Not too far away, seventeenth-century sailors swab the decks or repair the lines on the *Mayflower II*, while passengers discuss their worries surviving the first winter in the New World.

What It's Like to be a Character Interpreter

Jeremy Fried, in addition to his position as head of character interpreters at Williamsburg, has been interpreting the role of James Hubard, a colonial lawyer, off and on for the last 10 years.

Jeremy explains his job:

> My character spends most of his time in chambers, a fair-sized room in the courthouse, with a table in the middle seating 12 people. I sit down with a law book and quill and paper, and people come in and chat. But I don't work from a prepared script—that's what makes this form of interpretation different from other forms of living history.
>
> A character interpreter, often with the help of our various research depart-ments, examines the life of an eighteenth-century person by reading available documentation—personal letters, letters to the editor, newspapers. From this we can make inferences about their lives and what their beliefs were. As accurately as possible, we portray their ideas, their social knowledge and political opinions.
>
> Visitors ask questions about how "I" became a lawyer, about my family, about life in general in the eighteenth century. I've had people stay with me for one-and-a-half to two hours. This gets to be a bit of a challenge to stay in character. But I enjoy it.

Qualifications

Jeremy Fried stresses that the most important qualifications an applicant should possess are the ability to communicate with people, a pleasing personality and an inquisitive mind.

These requirements generally hold true for all living history museums throughout the country.

Jeremy Fried further explains: "Of course the foundation prefers people with a history major, but the flip side is, unless you've done your master's thesis on colonial Virginian society, you're still going to have to do the research. You could have only a GED but still be able to formulate ideas and coordinate information.

"We have a number of folks with history degrees, but we also have a retired florist and a former petty officer in the navy. It's a mixed bag of backgrounds. I have a degree in theater from the American Academy of Dramatic Arts in New York."

In addition, candidates would have to be the appropriate age and sex for a particular character they might be asked to play.

Jeremy points out one other qualification: "An applicant would have to be willing to accept a pretty low pay range."

Salaries

A full-time entry-level character interpreter earns between $7.50 and $9.50 an hour. But although it's an hourly wage, employees are given full benefits. Most contracts are for a 10-month period. A percentage of employees are laid off for two months during the winter, then rehired.

Offsetting the low salaries, Jeremy Fried points out, is that the people really enjoy working for the foundation.

"It's a nice work environment," Fried says. "The biggest stress is being hospitable to folks on vacation, and that's not a bad situation."

Salaries vary from site to site, of course, but most generally follow the same range offered in Williamsburg.

Hours

Most full-time employees put in an eight-hour day. At least four of those hours are spent in the characters' natural environment—in chambers, in class at the college, in their shops or homes. The rest of the time is spent moving around town, chatting with visitors, becoming a photo opportunity.

Ample time during the week is also allocated for research or to produce facsimile newspapers in the winter months.

Character interpreters at Plimoth Plantation attend to all the necessary tasks to keep the village thriving. They work in the fields, care for the farm animals (which have been "backbred" to resemble breeds from 300 years ago), and build new houses or repair existing ones.

Advancement

Opportunities occasionally come up to move into more administrative roles. A national association of interpreters has been newly formed to let people know that interpreting history is a highly specialized skill.

"Right now, though," Jeremy Fried admits, "the only way to advance is to get out of interpreting and into management."

How to Apply

A quick telephone call or letter will have an application on its way to you. Some sites even have job lines to tell you what positions are currently available. See Appendix C for more information.

Presenter

Jobs for presenters are much more numerous throughout the country than are character interpretation positions. Presenters differ from character interpreters in that most work from prepared scripts. Here acting ability is more important than research and ad-libbing skills.

Presenters generally reenact moments from history—a court scene, the Boston Tea Party, a fife-and-drum corps march—or other aspects of life in the historic site's particular period.

Sometimes, because enough information is not available for a particular place or people—the native people in seventeenth-century Plymouth, for example—a character interpreter would not be able to authentically take on a first-person role. Then presenters would explain to visitors what is known about the time in the third person. Presenters usually perform outfitted in authentic costumes.

Salaries for presenters are generally low and employment can often be seasonal, but the rewards of discussing your favorite place or time in history often compensate for the downsides.

Costumer

Most living history museums employ professional costumers to keep their character interpreters and presenters outfitted in authentic period clothing. Costumers generally work behind the scenes, reproducing the apparel the average inhabitant would have worn.

What It's Like to be a Costumer at Plimoth Plantation

Patricia Baker is wardrobe and textiles manager at Plimoth Plantation, a living history museum which has recreated the year 1627, seven years after the arrival of the *Mayflower* at Plymouth Rock. Her office and work space occupy a section of a converted dairy barn on the grounds of the museum. The atmosphere is that of a cozy living room with lots of shelves, fabrics draped here and there, sewing machines and rocking chairs, a large cutting table, garment racks, and a radio.

Patricia discusses her job:

The clothes my department makes are common to what the middle class would have worn. We provide interpreters with enough clothing so they can dress authentically from the skin out. They don't even have to wear modern underwear if they don't want to.

The basic undergarment for both men and women is a shift. It's a long, linen, T-shaped garment that reaches to the knees. Over that the men wear breeches and a doublet, a close-fitting jacket which comes to just above the waist. The breeches are tied into the jacket by laces.

Women wear a plain corset over their shift. It gives them a smooth, cone-shaped look. Next come a number of petticoats and skirts and a padded roll to enhance their hips. Waistlines are raised and meet in a point.

We use wool and linen and a little cotton, all naturally dyed. We try to duplicate the same materials used in the seventeenth-century, as well as the same construction techniques. Much of the sewing is done by hand.

We also make all the household furnishings that are used for display in the various exhibits. These are the seventeenth-century equivalents to what we have in the twentieth century: sheets, pillowcases (called pillow beres), feather and straw beds, paneled bed curtains, tablecloths, napkins, and cupboard cloths.

Maintaining and repairing existing costumes and furnishings are also part of our duties, as well as conducting as much research as possible to keep our creations accurate for the particular time period.

Because there are so few surviving garments—conditions were very harsh in those early years—we look to different sources: paintings, engravings, wood cuts, written descriptions, wills, inventories, diaries, and plays.

We also study the few remaining garments on display in different museums through our extensive slide collection of styles and techniques. Most of those museums are in England, the Victoria and Albert or the Museum of Costumes in Bath, for example. The clothing seems to have had a better survival rate over there.

Background

Patricia graduated from the Massachusetts College of Art in 1976 with a Bachelor of Fine Arts degree in crafts. Her concentration was in fabrics and fibers.

She immediately began work at Plimoth Plantation as a character interpreter. She joined the wardrobe department in 1985
and became its head the following year.

How to Get Started

The wardrobe department at Plimoth Plantation is a small one,
currently employing only four workers. Other larger living history
museums, such as Colonial Williamsburg, need more people. A
good way to get a foot in the door is to apply for an apprenticeship,
internship, or work-study position.

Salaries

A new graduate just starting out could expect an annual salary in
the $17,000 to $26,000 range, depending on the location and
available funding.

The Historic Trades

Most living history museums employ skilled artisans to demonstrate early crafts and trades. Some of these artisans perform in
the first person, playing the role of a particular character of the
time. Others wear twentieth-century clothing and discuss their
craft from a modern perspective.

In the stores and workshops lining the Duke of Gloucester and
Francis streets in Colonial Williamsburg, you will find harness
makers, milliners, tailors, needleworkers, silversmiths, apothecar-
ies, candle makers, bookbinders, printers, and wig makers. In the
Pilgrim Village and Crafts Center at Plimoth Plantation there are
coopers, blacksmiths, joiners (cabinet makers), potters, and basket makers and weavers.

In addition to giving demonstrations, artisans often produce many of the items used on display in the various exhibits. This includes the furniture, cookware, and even sometimes the actual buildings.

Interpretive Artisans at Plimoth Plantation

Most of the items the Pilgrims used in 1627 were brought with them on the *Mayflower*, or imported later. Because the Pilgrim Village at Plimoth Plantation is time-specific to the year 1627, only those crafts which were practiced then are demonstrated there. In addition to their principal occupation as farmers, 1627 pilgrims were coopers, blacksmiths, thatchers, and house builders. The interpretive artisans perform in costume and play the role of a designated Pilgrim documented to have lived in Plymouth during that year.

Being a Cooper at Plimoth Plantation

Tom Gerhardt interprets the character of one of the most famous pilgrims, John Alden, a cooper who worked both inside a one-room cottage he shared with his wife and two children and outside in the adjoining yard.

Tom talks about his job:

I make barrels and other different-sized wooden containers, such as buckets and churns, while answering visitors' questions about life in seventeenth-century Plymouth.

Although in Europe you could still find people practicing the craft as it once was done, there are only a few barrel makers in this country. Wooden barrels are made mostly for the wine and spirits industry, but now it's a mechanized craft using power tools and machinery. The finished product is the same as the old craft, but the method is different. We practice the craft as it was done in the 1600s, using only hand tools.

In addition to my duties as an interpretive cooper, I am also responsible for general woodworking. I am one of several Pilgrims building a new house on the grounds.

What I enjoy most about Plimoth Plantation is that there are a number of very creative and talented people here. If you're willing to do the work, you can learn a good deal for yourself, while at the same time you're educating the visitors.

There are so many people who will help you—you can be inspired by what they're doing; and you have the time to explore and develop your skills.

Background

Tom Gerhardt's interest in history began as a small child. His father was a volunteer in charge of a small museum in Virginia, and he took the family on vacations all over the country visiting other museums. It was on one of these trips Tom first discovered Plimoth Plantation.

Later, Tom took a few courses under a master cooper in Portsmouth, New Hampshire, and went to college for a couple of years, studying general liberal arts and theater. He worked in the technical end of theater for awhile but decided he wanted a change. Since he'd always been interested in the recreation of history, in 1985 he came back to Plimoth Plantation and applied for a job as an interpreter.

Working in the Crafts Center at Plimoth Plantation

Plimoth Plantation also operates a Crafts Center where other seventeenth-century crafts are demonstrated. Potters, joiners, basket makers, weavers, and a gift shop share space in a converted carriage house. Artisans in the Crafts Center wear twentieth-century clothing and discuss their work from a modern viewpoint.

Being a Joiner in the Crafts Center

Joel Pontz is the supervisor of all interpretive artisans at Plimoth Plantation as well as character interpreter for a farmer, John Adams. He also demonstrates his joinery skills in the Crafts Center.

Joel describes his job:

I step back and forth between the seventeenth and the twentieth centuries. Several days a week I'm in costume in the Village as John Adams, picking my share of rutabagas or building small animal shelters or fences. On the other days I'm in modern clothing in the Crafts Center, demonstrating joinery.

Joiners were the principal furniture makers of the period, in the age before cabinetry. We use different kinds of saws and edged hand tools, such as axes, planes, gimlets, and augers, rather than power tools. If we want to reproduce the right texture or style, we have to be purists about it.

In the Craft Center, in front of the public or behind the scenes, we make furniture for the village—large cupboards, bedsteads, chairs, mousetraps, and children's toys. We don't want to demonstrate any crafts in the Village section of the museum that weren't practiced at the time. It would be anachronistic.

Background

Joel Pontz grew up nearby and started at Plimoth Plantation as a volunteer Pilgrim after school and on weekends. In 1973 he became a full-time character interpreter.

He learned his joinery skill on site, from the other staff members and the research department.

"I hated woodworking in school," Joel admits. "It wasn't until I started working at the plantation, using hand tools and trying to decipher how things were made, that it became actually interesting for me. The historical aspect of it was what fascinated me. If it were just doing straight carpentry, I probably wouldn't have stayed with it."

How to Get Started

Joel advises taking a few courses in historic trades or historic preservation. "But," he cautions, "the skills we need are particular to Plimoth Plantation. Outside courses would be painted with such a broad brush, but what's done at Plimoth Plantation is very focused on a particular group of people in a very short time span.

"The best qualification would be a lot of hand-tool work. The tools haven't changed that much over the centuries. Try taking a tree and make a table or a chair from it. That's the best way to learn the art."

Because of limited budgets and a low turnover, openings are rare. However, they do take on interns occasionally, and there is a volunteer program that could help you get your foot in the door.

Being a Potter in the Crafts Center

In the Crafts Center at Plimoth Plantation, four potters demonstrate the art of seventeenth-century throwing techniques, though only one potter is on duty at a time. They also make all the pieces that are used in the Village by the interpreters. During the winter months when the museum is closed to visitors, the potters make enough items to replenish their stock.

Deb Mason has her own home studio, where she teaches pottery classes, does commission work, and makes pieces for display at various galleries. She also spends two eight-hour days a week in the Crafts Center and is the supervisor of the other potters.

Deb talks about her job:

In the Crafts Center we don't claim to be seventeenth-century people because pottery wasn't done in the Village in 1627. But because of this, we have an advantage. We can talk to visitors in a way that's totally different from the interpreters. A visitor might go to the Village, then come back to the Crafts Center to ask a question that the seventeenth-century interpreters couldn't answer. The interpreters have to speak as though they are Pilgrims. They wouldn't have any knowledge beyond 1627.

For now we are working with twentieth-century equipment, though we are discussing the possibility of going back in time, using a kick wheel and a wood-burning stove. The electric wheels we use now might make throwing look faster and easier than it was in the seventeenth century, but the techniques are still very much the same.

The difference is we have to make only period pieces, and there some of the difficulties come in. For example, we're trying to find the right clay bodies to work with. We have a few original pieces on display to study, and you can see the clay color and texture. We've been experimenting, trying to develop clay bodies that are close to the original.

That's been fairly successful; but we're having a tough time with glazes. They used a lot of lead back then. In fact, most every glaze was lead-based. Because we sell the pieces we make in the gift shop and they're also used in the Village every day, we've been trying to get away from lead. It's hard to come up with glazes that have the same shine and the same colors; lead has a very typical look.

We're using a ground glass that melts at a low temperature, which is a characteristic of lead, and produces similar results.

We make ointment pots that held salves and other healing lotions, apothecary jars, bowls, porringers for porridge, oil lamps, candlesticks, and pipkins, a little cooking pot with a side handle and three legs on the bottom. We also make a lot of three-handled cups. Pilgrims usually shared their eating implements. The cups are funny-looking things—a popular item in the craft shop.

Back then the pottery was hastily thrown. There's a real earthy quality to the pieces. Their perception of what was beautiful and what was utilitarian was different. What they strove for was extremely rough by today's standards.

My biggest problem is remembering not to throw too well. The advantage to that, though, for potters wanting to work here, is that a high degree of skill is not necessary.

Background

Deb Mason earned her B.A. in Art with a major in ceramics in 1973 from Bennington College in Vermont. She taught ceramics full time for 13 years at a private school and was the head of the art department her last few years there. She joined the staff at Plimoth Plantation in 1992.

Salaries

Salaries for craftworkers differ depending on whether they are full time or part time. The latter group earns an hourly wage ranging between $7.50 and $10.

Researcher

Researchers are the backbone behind every living history museum. Without their efforts, the ability to recreate authentic period characters, to accurately restore historic buildings, or to reproduce a facsimile of daily life would be an impossible task.

Carolyn Travers is director of research at Plimoth Plantation. Carolyn talks about her job:

We have four sites at Plimoth Plantation: the 1627 Pilgrim Village; the *Mayflower II;* Hobbamock's Homesite, a Wampanohg Indian site; and the Carriage House Crafts Center. We research anything we need for our program, from what is the period attitude toward toads, how a character felt about being her husband's third wife, the correct way to cook a particular dish, to some obscure point of Calvinist theology. The women are more difficult to research than the men because there is less documented information on them. You are forced into recreating a more typical persona than the actual character, sort of a generic portrayal. In general, we research the life and genealogical background and social history for all the characters we portray.

In our research we use a variety of sources—court records and genealogical research done by professional genealogists such as the General Society of Mayflower Descendants, or writers for the *American Genealogist* or other genealogy periodicals.

We also have researchers in other departments. For example, the authenticity of buildings and structures is done more by our curatorial department.

Background

Carolyn attended Earlham College, a small Quaker school in Richmond, Indiana, where she earned a B.A. degree in fine arts with a concentration in history. She then went on to Simmons Graduate School of Library and Information Science in Boston and graduated in 1981 with an MS in LIS (Master's in Library and Information Science) with a concentration in research methods.

Carolyn grew up in Plymouth and started work at the age of 14 as a part-time Pilgrim. After she finished her master's degree, she returned to Plimoth Plantation as a researcher.

Qualifications

Carolyn points out that researching is a competitive field, and that a higher degree, in history or library science with a research methods concentration, is necessary.

A candidate is not expected to have a general body of knowledge about the specific time period, but he or she must have strong research skills, talent, and experience.

Salaries

New graduates might begin with a yearly salary as low as $14,000. "You don't do it for the money," Carolyn stresses. "There are a lot of psychological payments. One of the satisfactions is to be able to change someone's mind about the stereotypes surrounding early colonists."

Researchers can find work in a variety of other settings as well: university archeology and history departments, preservation boards, libraries and archives, government offices, and history museums.

Other Jobs at Living History Museums

The following is a list of other job categories found in living history museums. Many are discussed in detail in later chapters.

Architecture
Archeology
Business Affairs
Building and Grounds Maintenance
Collections Management
Curatorship
Development and Membership

Educational Programs
Information
Personnel
Public Relations
Sales
Security
Visitor Services

CHAPTER THREE

The National Park Service
Working with Our National Treasures

T he National Park Service, a bureau under the U.S. Department of the Interior, administers more than 160 natural and recreational areas across the country, including the Grand Canyon, Yellowstone National Park, and Lake Mead.

Another 200 sites of cultural and historic significance fall under the park service's jurisdiction and offer numerous employment opportunities of interest to history buffs.

Most history-related jobs are located in the mid-Atlantic, southeast, and national capital regions; most archeology-related positions are in the West and Southwest. The various sites encompass battlefields, national monuments, historical and military parks, forts, and memorials.

Because most sites are not located near major cities, serious candidates must, for the most part, be prepared to relocate. Housing may or may not be provided, depending upon the site and your position.

Park Ranger (Interpretation)

The National Park Service hires three categories of park rangers (generally on a seasonal basis): enforcement, general, and interpretation. Most history buffs apply for positions in the latter category.

Duties vary greatly from position to position and site to site, but rangers in the interpretation division are usually responsible for developing and presenting programs that explain a park's historic, cultural, or archeological features. This is done through talks, demonstrations, and guided walking tours. Rangers also sit at information desks, provide visitor services, or participate in conservation or restoration projects. Entry-level employees might also collect fees, provide first aid, and operate audiovisual equipment.

Qualifications and Salaries

In determining a candidate's eligibility for employment, and at which salary level he or she would be placed, the National Park Service weighs several factors. In essence, those with the least experience or education will begin at the lowest federal government salary grade of GS-2. But the requirements for that grade are only six months of experience in related work or a high school diploma or its equivalent.

The more relevant work experience or education, the higher the salary level. For example, GS-4 requires 18 months of general experience in park operations or in related fields and 6 months of specialized experience; or one 90-day season as a seasonal park ranger at the GS-3 level.

Completion of two academic years of college may be substituted for experience if the course work covers social science, history, archeology, parks and recreation management, or other related disciplines.

Close-up: St. Augustine—America's Oldest City

From an aerial vantage point or entering from the south across the Bridge of Lions (named for the Spanish explorer Ponce de

Leon), St. Augustine, Florida, America's Oldest City, resembles a European burg, a medieval hamlet. Fairy-tale castles with spires and turrets rise above the roofs of gingerbread-trimmed doll-houses. Horse-drawn carriages, stone walls, city gates, and a coquina block fort add to the fanciful effect.

Reputedly one of the oldest roadways in the oldest city in the country, St. George Street was fully restored in the mid-1970s. On either side of the narrow promenade, signs adorn vintage buildings proclaiming the Oldest Wooden School House, built during the first Spanish occupation before the American Revolution, the Oldest Pharmacy, and the Oldest Store, with a collection of more than 100,000 of yesterday's mementos.

St. Augustine's Oldest House is one of the most-studied and best documented houses in the United States. It was originally built with palm thatchings covering a crude structure of logs and boards, then restored after a fire in 1702 with coquina walls and tapia flooring (a mixture of lime, shell, and sand). The house provides a record of life in St. Augustine for over 400 years. In spite of raids, looting, and fire, archeologists—through digs and research—have shown continuous occupancy of the site dating from the early 1600s to the present day.

Nearby, the Authentic Old Jail, listed in the National Register of Historic Places, contains the original weapons used in crimes and offers an interesting courtyard display. The building, with living quarters for the sheriff and his family, served the county until 1953.

South of the Old City Gate is St. Augustine's Spanish Quarter. In this living history museum are restored homes and gardens over 250 years old. Guides and artisans dressed in period clothing recreate the daily lifestyle, giving visitors an inside look at life for eighteenth-century soldiers and settlers.

Castillo de San Marcos National Monument, built by the Spanish between 1672 and 1695, and now run by the National Park Service, is dubbed America's Oldest Fort. It took more than 50 years after Ponce de Leon claimed *La Florida* for Spain to establish a permanent settlement in St. Augustine. The early Spaniards had many clashes with colonialists in neighboring Georgia and North and South Carolina. St. Augustine was burned to the ground twice. The fort was finally constructed to secure the city.

Lacking brick-making materials, the Spanish used blocks of coquina, a native shellstone quarried locally across the bay on Anastasia Island. Softer than brick, it helped the fort withstand numerous attacks, its walls absorbing the impact of iron cannon balls rather than shattering the way brick would.

The coquina tends to break off when touched, and portions of the fort have been eroding away. The damage is irreparable; a mortar substitute can be used to patch up the surface here and there, but park rangers warn visitors not to lean against the walls.

The fort raised different flags above its walls many times during the years, through wartime and peace, through treaties, trades and negotiations, but in 1821 it changed hands for the last time when the United States acquired Florida from Spain.

The fort is also significant in that it houses what claim to be the Nation's Oldest Toilets.

Further Reading
America's First City: St. Augustine's Historic Neighborhoods, by Karen Harvey, illustrated by Nina McGuire, Tailored Tours Publications.

What It's Like to Be a Park Ranger at Castillo de San Marcos

Gordie Wilson graduated college in 1977 with a degree in parks and recreation and immediately began working for the National Park Service. Today, in addition to his post as superintendent of Castillo de San Marcos National Monument, he is also in charge of nearby Fort Matanzas National Monument.

Gordie talks about the duties of a park ranger:

There really is no such thing as a typical day. Duties are varied and there is always the unexpected. A park ranger might begin the day sitting at the ticket booth collecting fees, then go inside the fort to give a two-hour presentation to visitors, explaining the fort's history. Later, costumed park rangers set off the cannons in a daily display, while others ensure that would-be treasure hunters are not defacing the property with shovels and metal detectors.

If a visitor has a heart attack, which is not a rare occurrence, then trained park rangers will administer CPR or other forms of first aid. A park ranger must be prepared to take on a variety of duties.

Getting Your Foot in the Door in the National Park Service

"Competition for jobs, especially at the most well-known sites, can be fierce," Gordie Wilson explains, "but the National Park Service employs a huge permanent staff, and this is supplemented tenfold by an essential seasonal work force during peak visitation periods.

"The best way for a newcomer to break in is to start off with seasonal employment during school breaks. With a couple of summer seasons under your belt, the doors will open more easily for permanent employment."

And, because of Office of Personnel Management regulations, veterans of the U.S. armed forces have a decided advantage. Depending upon their experience, they may be given preference among applicants.

How to Apply

Recruitment for summer employment begins September 1, with a January 15 deadline. Some sites, such as Death Valley or Everglades National Park, also have a busy winter season. The winter recruitment period is June 1 through July 15.

Applications for seasonal employment with the National Park Service can be obtained through the Office of Personnel Management or by writing to:

U.S. Department of the Interior
National Park Service
Seasonal Employment Unit
P.O. Box 37127
Washington, DC 20013-7127

You may also contact one of the ten regional offices of the National Park Service. Their addresses are listed in Appendix B.

Historian

In addition to park ranger positions, the National Park Service has another category called, simply, historian. Duties involve conducting research and producing inventories and reports on specific sites, structures, and technical processes.

Historians also work with the National Register of Historic Places, which is a branch of the Interagency Resources Division administered by the National Park Service.

The National Register of Historic Places

The National Register of Historic Places is the United States' official list of national resources worthy of preservation. Part of a national program, the National Register of Historic Places supports public and private efforts to identify, evaluate, and protect America's historic and archeological resources.

The National Register includes all historic areas in the National Park System, National Historic Landmarks designated by the secretary of the interior, and properties such as historic districts, sites, buildings, structures, and objects significant in American history, architecture, archeology, engineering, and culture.

There are over 2,000 nominations put forward each year; the vast majority meet all eligibility requirements and are entered in the National Register. Here are a few interesting recent listings:

PROPERTY	SIGNIFICANCE
The Moulin Rouge Hotel in Las Vegas, Nevada	Of exceptional importance in the history of integration: first club built (1955) to cater to an integrated audience.
The Ma Rainey House, home to Gertrude Pridgett "Ma" Rainey, nicknamed Mother of the Blues, Columbus, Georgia	For her contribution to the world of music.
The Luber School in Stone County, in the Arkansas Ozarks	A one-room stone building remarkable as a monument to educational reforms both in Arkansas and nationally.
The ruins of "Galloping Gertie," a collapsed suspension bridge submerged in Puget Sound near Tacoma, Washington	The bridge's failure ushered in new developments in bridge design and aerodynamics.
The Eric Ellis Soderholtz Cottage, home to the noted potter and photographer, West Guildsboro, Maine.	Built by the artist, it's one of the state's most distinctive arts and crafts cottages and an important example of Craftsman architecture in rural America.

Admission to the National Register of Historic Places brings national recognition and various tax benefits—and federal grants for historic preservation when funds are available. Nominations usually begin on the local and state level, by individuals and agencies, then are submitted to the National Register for Historic Places for final review.

The National Register of Historic Places employs about 12 full-time professional historians, architectural historians, and archeologists. Historian Antoinette Lee has been with the National Register since November of 1989.

Antoinette discusses her job:

> I coordinate our National Register program. We produce a lot of technical information on evaluating properties for the National Register. I handle public accessibility by promoting the National Register's Starter Kit through advertisements. The kit is helpful to people considering nominating a property. I also issue press releases on new monthly listings.
>
> All the historians are assigned different regions in the country; I am responsible for the register's programs in the western states. I evaluate the nominations to the register that come in, then admit them if they're eligible.
>
> We participate in different workshops and seminars and get out in the field occasionally to meet people on the front line of historic preservation at the state and local levels.

Background

Antoinette's interest in history was largely influenced by her grandmother, who in the 1920s and '30s worked toward the preservation of Pullman, Illinois—George Pullman's railway community.

Antoinette has well over 20 years of experience in the field. She earned a B.A. degree in history at the University of Pennsylvania, and her Ph.D. in American civilization from George Washington University in Washington, D.C.

During the bicentennial era in the 1970s, she did a lot of free-lance research work for various historians, architectural historians, and preservationists who were involved in major studies commemorating the 1976 bicentennial. One of her projects was a history of state capitol buildings. In the late 1970s and early 1980s, she worked for the National Trust for Historic Preservation, which is a private, nonprofit preservation organization, as education coordinator.

After that she worked for eight years as a private consultant in historic preservation. When a friend showed her the announcement for the position of historian with the National Register for Historic Places, Antoinette applied by filling out the Standard Form 171 and was selected.

What It Takes to Be a Historian

A candidate for the position of historian should be willing to serve the public and should have an understanding of history at all its levels—national, state and local. It is also important to be aware of the preservation needs of the public and to be able to help people in achieving their goals.

To quality for a historian position, which merits a federal government rating of GS-5 through GS-15, applicants must have least a B.A. in architectural history, history of technology, American civilization, historic preservation, or a related field. A graduate degree is preferred. Several years worth of field experience is also important in order to be able to adequately evaluate nominated properties.

For current salary information for these grades, check with the Office of Personnel Management (there are offices in most major cities) or with any federal agency.

Getting a Foot in the Door

Paid internships are available through the National Council for Preservation Education, but the number of internships available is relatively small. There are generally numerous job and internship opportunities at the state and local levels. You can start your investigations at your local library.

For more information call or write:

The National Register of Historic Places
U.S. Department of the Interior
National Park Service
P.O. Box 37127
Washington, DC 20013-7127
(202) 343-9536

CHAPTER FOUR

History Museums
Displaying the Past

N othing makes history come more alive than to hold a piece of it in your hands. From acquiring collections and preserving them, to explaining and displaying them, in history museums history buffs have the chance to work with every aspect of the relics and other forms of physical evidence of the past.

There are thousands of history museums across the country. They are housed in purpose-built structures or in historic buildings and homes open to the public.

Many are large enterprises employing scores of professionals to handle day-to-day operations. Other museums are small and operate with only a handful of employees and dedicated volunteers.

The larger the museum, the more specialized an employee's duties are. Professionals in mid-size or small museums must be willing to take on a variety of tasks. However, knowledge of or familiarity with all areas of museum functions, in addition to a strong background in a particular discipline, are important qualifications for any staff member.

Along with the proper educational achievements, the American Association of Museums (AAM) suggests these additional qualifications for museum personnel:

A museum professional should be expected to have a familiarity with the history, goals, and functions of museums; a knowledge of and commitment to the AAM statement on ethics; and a willingness to improve skills by study and by attendance at training sessions, seminars, and professional conferences.

Dedication, integrity, diplomacy, and a commitment to thoroughness and accuracy are demanded of all museum professionals. The ability to communicate orally and in writing and to work constructively with associates is essential.

An awareness of legal issues affecting museums, and the ability to prepare and interpret budgets and grant applications are required of all positions. Additional knowledge, skills, and abilities such as a second language, typing and word processing, and familiarity with the museum's community and its resources may be required for certain positions and are always beneficial and desirable.

The AAM has identified dozens of direct and museum-related career categories. Several of those of interest to history lovers are examined here, along with the expected requirements for levels of education, experience, knowledge, abilities, and skills.

Collections Manager

The collections manager supervises, numbers, catalogs, and stores the specimens within each division of the museum.

EDUCATION REQUIREMENTS At least an undergraduate degree in the area of the museum's specialization. An advanced degree in museum studies with a concentration in a specific discipline is recommended.

EXPERIENCE At least three years experience in a museum registration department or in a position in which the main duties are the technical aspects of handling, storage, preservation, and cataloging.

KNOWLEDGE AND SKILLS Knowledge of information management techniques. Ability to accurately identify objects within the museum's collection. Knowledge of security practices and environmental controls.

Curator

Curators are specialists in a particular academic discipline relevant to a museum's collections. They are generally responsible for the care and interpretation of all objects and specimens on loan or belonging to the museum, and they are fully knowledgeable about each object's history and importance.

Depending upon the museum and their area of interest, curators can work with textiles and costumes, paintings, memorabilia, historic structures, crafts, furniture, coins, or a variety of other historically significant items.

EDUCATION REQUIREMENTS   A curator would normally possess an advanced degree with a concentration in an area related to the museum's collections.

EXPERIENCE   Three years of experience in a museum or related educational or research facility would usually be required before a candidate could advance to a full curatorial position.

KNOWLEDGE AND SKILLS   Ability to explain and interpret the collection to the public. Being familiar with the techniques of selection, evaluation, preservation, restoration, and exhibition of the museum's collection.

Director

A museum director must have specialized knowledge of the museum's collections and be responsible for acquisitions, preservation, research, and presentation. A director also must be familiar with policy making, handling funding and budgets, supervising staff, and coordinating museum activities.

EDUCATION REQUIREMENTS An advanced degree in the area of the museum's specialty is required, with coursework in museum administration.

EXPERIENCE Three years or more management experience in a museum or related institution.

KNOWLEDGE AND SKILLS A director should have specialized knowledge of at least one area of the museum's collections or in the management of the particular type of museum. His or her area of expertise must also include implementing policies and financial planning.

Educator

An educator's main function is to enhance public awareness of and access to the museum's collections. To do this, an educator designs and implements programs encompassing a variety of media and techniques and arranges for special events, workshops, and teacher training programs. In addition, an educator might train docents and tour guides and might have other supervisory and administrative duties.

EDUCATION REQUIREMENTS An advanced degree in education, museum education, or an area of the museum's specialization.

EXPERIENCE Two years in a museum education department or other related facility.

KNOWLEDGE AND SKILLS Ability to prepare material for publications and exhibitions. Skills in oral and written communication. Knowledge of school systems' curricula and research techniques.

Exhibit Designer

The exhibit designer works closely with curatorial and educational personnel to convey ideas into permanent or temporary exhibits. They use drawings, scale models, special lighting, and other techniques. An exhibit designer can have administrative responsibilities and may supervise the production of exhibits.

EDUCATION REQUIREMENTS A degree or certification in graphic or industrial design, commercial art or communications arts, architecture, interior design, or studio arts.

EXPERIENCE Experience in exhibition design and related construction work with wood, metal, or plastics. A portfolio of past and current work is necessary.

KNOWLEDGE AND SKILLS Ability to conceptualize exhibit designs, and skill in mechanical drawing, making refined esthetic judgments, and supervising installation of exhibits.

The Smithsonian Institution

When most Americas think about spending a day at the mall, they've got shopping 'til they drop on their mind. But residents of and seasoned visitors to Washington, D.C., know that the Mall, located between the U.S. Capitol and the Washington Monument, is a nicely manicured strip of land housing nine museums of the Smithsonian Institution complex. The Smithsonian also has six other museums and galleries—two are located in New York—as well as the National Zoological Park.

The museums are named here:

Anacostia Museum

Arthur M. Sackler Gallery

Arts and Industries Building

Cooper Hewitt Museum (New York)

Freer Gallery of Art

Hirshhorn Museum and Sculpture Garden

National Air and Space Museum

National Museum of African Art

National Museum of American Art

National Museum of American History

National Museum of the American Indian (slated to move to Washington, D.C. from New York in the mid- to late 1990s)

National Museum of Natural History

National Portrait Gallery

Renwick Gallery

Smithsonian Institution Building (the Castle)

The chief executive officer of the Smithsonian is given the title of secretary. The institution is governed by a board of regents which, by law, is composed of the vice president of the United States, the chief justice of the United States, three members of the Senate, three members of the House of Representatives, and nine private citizen members. Traditionally, the chief justice of the United States has served as chancellor of the museum.

The Castle houses the Smithsonian's central administration offices. Each individual museum has its own director and staff.

The National Museum of American History, part of the Smithsonian Institution complex on the National Mall, is devoted to the exhibition, care, and study of artifacts that reflect the experience of the American people. The museum receives more than 5 million visitors a year. It has the responsibility for preserving the more than 16 million objects it has acquired over the last century, and it has more than 430 employees on staff.

Meet a Curator at the National Museum of American History

Charles McGovern is supervisor of the American History Museum's division of Community Life, overseeing a group of technicians, specialists, collection-based researchers, curators, and support staff. He is also a curator, responsible for Twentieth-Century Consumerism and Popular Culture. This department covers the history of entertainment, leisure, recreation, and commerce.

The exhibits within this department are probably the most popular and the most well-known. Visitors to the museum come to view Judy Garland's ruby slippers from the *Wizard of Oz*; Caroll O'Connor's well-worn chair used by his character, Archie Bunker, on "All in the Family"; or ventriloquist Edgar Bergen's famous wooden dummy, Charlie McCarthy.

Charles' interest in cultural history began at an early age. He watched a lot of television and listened to the radio and participated in the mass popular culture in the 1960s. His father and mother told him about the times when they were growing up, sharing with him stories about the early days of radio. When Charles got to high school and read books his teachers recommended, he realized that Babe Ruth and Laurel and Hardy and the Marx brothers, personalities he cared very deeply about, were as much a part of history as Calvin Coolidge or the First World War.

Charles talks about his job:

Part of my profession as an historian is to be a decoder or an explainer, to go back into the heads and the lives and the beliefs of our ancestors. And here, we try to do that respectfully, understanding the world as they saw it. As we do that, we see how culture reflects the times, the fears and ideals and problems of a given society. You cannot look at certain creations of our popular culture without seeing those kinds of elements in them.

As a curator, I am responsible for the creation and maintenance of the collections in my subject area. I document the history of the everyday life of American people. The major outline for my job puts me in charge of building collections, developing exhibitions, conducting research, writing, public service, public speaking, and being a graduate advisor to 11 research fellows.

Specifically, my job is divided into three parts: acquisitions—acquiring new objects and exhibits for the museum; exhibiting and interpreting; and research.

The collections I am responsible for include a lot of the things related to the history of American entertainment: a hat that Jimmy Durante used in his stage appearances, Ann Miller's tap shoes, Howdy Doody, Mr. Moose and Bunny Rabbit and the Grandfather clock from Captain Kangaroo, the suit of armor worn by Francis X. Bushman in the original 1936 movie, *Ben Hur*, Carol Burnett's char lady costume, Mister Rogers' sweater, Harrison Ford's *Indiana Jones* outfit (his leather jacket and hat), Tom Selleck's ring from "Magnum, P.I." and his Hawaiian shirt and baseball cap, old 78 rpm records, movie posters, and comic books. We also look for collections that give us insight into American consumerism and commerce. We have the bonnet that was worn by the woman who posed for the Sunmaid raisin box, a huge collection of turn-of-the-century advertising, marketing and packaging items from the Hills Bros. Coffee Company, and a collection of memorabilia from World's Fairs from 1851 to 1988.

To build our collections, we depend largely on people donating items. In fact, almost everything has been donated. We have very little money in our acquisitions budget. We can't compete in a very inflated market with the galleries and people who deal with "collectibles." People must be willing to donate, so we look for people who either don't need the money or get the point of what we're trying to do.

Sometimes we're not able to accept everything that is being offered. Someone called once and wanted to donate Charlie Chaplin's cane. But first, how do I know it was his cane? It's impossible to document that. And second, Chaplin probably went through thousands of canes. Those bamboo things snapped very easily. Something like that we couldn't take.

And although I must be familiar with every piece's history, the range and variety of items I am responsible for is staggering. It's not as if I were a curator of painting where I'm trained in oils and brush techniques. Once in awhile I have to confer with an appraiser or dealer to determine authenticity.

Once a donation has been accepted, we can never promise that it will go on display. Less than 2 percent of our collection is on display at any given time, the rest is kept in storage. Although some exhibits, such as the ruby slippers or Archie's chair, are permanent, others rotate.

Part of my job is to decide what gets exhibited, what gets stored, what is rotated. And to care for all the items, to make sure they don't deteriorate, we need to remove even permanent exhibits from time to time. People travel a long way expecting to see a certain item, and if it's not on display they're usually upset. They don't realize they should check with us first if they're coming to see something in particular. We took Charlie McCarthy off to clean him one day, and within a half an hour we had three phone calls saying where was Charlie McCarthy?

The exhibiting side of my job is really a team effort. Exhibit designers work with curators to decide *how* an item should be displayed. The designer is responsible for the layout of objects and text and graphics and props. A conservator, someone who takes care of the actual repair or maintenance of an object, would be responsible for the "prescription"—"This piece needs to be lit with not more than thirty footcandles," for example.

But I feel that research is really my first duty. All the collecting and exhibiting doesn't mean anything unless you have something to say. You have to figure out first what point you're making. Our point is the showing of everyday life of the American people, and for earlier times that's something that has to be researched. Of course you do research to support the things you already have in your collection, but the research also helps you to determine what you should be out there collecting.

Background

Charles studied at Swarthmore College in Pennsylvania and finished in 1980 with a B.A. with honors in history. He immediately began graduate school at Harvard and earned his Master's of Arts in history in 1983 and his Ph.D. in American civilization in 1993.

During that time, Charles taught history at Harvard, and then from 1986 through 1987 he served at the Smithsonian as a research fellow. In 1988 he became a full-time curator.

The Smithsonian as a Training Ground

Every year the Smithsonian awards dozens of research fellowships, providing funding to Ph.D. candidates and access to museum collections.

To be hired as a curator, candidates must have their Ph.D. or be almost finished with it. Entry-level positions include technicians and specialists and research-related jobs. Paid internships and volunteer positions are usually available and a good way to get a foot in the door.

Charles points out that jobs for curators at the Smithsonian seldom become available. But because the Smithsonian has a certain reputation and skill in training, it's a good place to gain a foundation and then go out to other areas or institutions for work. An internship at the Smithsonian will go a long way in securing employment elsewhere. He believes that because of the Smithsonian's size, sometimes really interesting work gets done in smaller museums with a more fixed mission.

Salaries

A beginning curator who has almost completed a Ph.D. would come in somewhere in the high $20,000s. The next jump would be to the mid-$30,000s. Staff at the Smithsonian are employees of the federal government and follow the GS scale.

Meet an Exhibit Designer at the National Museum of American History

Many small and even mid-size institutions do not have room in their budgets for a specialist exhibit designer. In a situation such as that, one or two people, the director or the curator, might perform the functions of an exhibit designer in addition to the duties of their own specialty. Or, in some cases, the museum will contract with an outside firm for exhibit design work.

The Smithsonian Institution, a large operation, employs over 20 exhibit designers and assistants; five of those designers work specifically for The National Museum of American History.

Hank Grasso is a senior exhibit designer working in all of the different departments within the National Museum of American History.

Hank came to the Smithsonian in 1990 as a visual information specialist, the government's position for an exhibit designer. He generally functions as part of a team of professionals including curators, collections managers, conservators, scriptwriters, audience advocates—or educators, as they are most often known—and project managers.

He came on board specifically to work with the American Encounters Show, the museum's Columbus quincentenary presentation, dealing with 500 years of history in America. He has also worked on the designs for the "Working People of Philadelphia" in the Life in America exhibit, Science in American Life, the East Broadtop Railroad, Manufactured Weather, and Feed Bags as Fashion, a popular exhibit on an unusual fashion trend.

Hank discusses the process of exhibit design:

> If you have 1,000 images and 10 square feet of space, you need to come up with a vehicle that will allow those images to be displayed. You can compress them into a video disk or a series of slide presentations, or storyboards. We look at the information we're wanting to convey, and then translate it visually, keeping an eye to spacial allocations.
>
> There are two distinct models you can follow. With the traditional model, the cast of characters involved stay in very rigid roles: the curator passes his abstract ideas over to the designer, who then translates them into a physical presentation. The curator is responsible for content and ideas and the written word, the designer is responsible for the environment and the esthetics and graphic design.
>
> A more modern approach is called a collaborative exhibition development, involving a team of professionals working together. We worked this way when we were creating the American Encounters show, a permanent exhibit at the Smithsonian. We created design tools so all parts of the team could understand each other. We could look over each other's shoulders and know what we were seeing.

Putting an Exhibit Together

These are just a few of the many steps a collaborative team follows when working on a new exhibit:

1. Listen to ideas, identify interpretive goals. Why are we telling this story? What is the most important message we want to convey?

2. Look at the available space and create a floor plan.

3. Combine steps 1 and 2 by prioritizing ideas and looking at the elements that will hold the exhibit together.

4. Decide how it will be done—presentation vehicles, techniques, and technology.

5. Choose the objects and images that will best tell the story.

6. Make a scale model rendering all the individual objects and labels and graphic images.

7. Translate design control drawings, sets of drawings that have to do with the general contracting and building of spaces and with the making of exhibit parts.

8. Write the script and labels for the exhibit.

9. Begin the competitive bid process for general contracting.

10. Construct a full-scale model.

11. Conduct audience research. How does the audience react? Can they understand the material and the ideas being presented?

12. Do final construction.

13. Handle promotional and outreach elements.

Background

Hank attended Denison University, a small liberal arts school in Ohio, from 1972 to 1974. During his two years there, he had a chance to get a good overview of the various courses and decide what he wanted to pursue. He then transferred to Penn State and studied in the wood products division, specializing in wood as an art medium, looking at both its esthetic and structural uses. He also combined his study of wood products with courses in the architecture department, including drafting and drawing, and graduated in 1976 with a B.A. in interdisciplinary studies. He later went back to school at Pratt Institute in New York and took graduate courses to increase his conceptualization skills and learn more about different fabricating techniques.

Between his time at Penn State and Pratt, Hank worked for a couple of different private design firms which were contracted by various museums. While building up his portfolio, Hank had an opportunity to work on exhibit designs for the John F. Kennedy Library in Boston, the Basketball Hall of Fame, the Bowling Hall of Fame, the New York Historical Society, the United Nations, the Metropolitan Museum of Art, the Frederick Douglas Place, and the Buffalo Bill Historical Center.

Getting on the Right Path

Today there are three main educational preparation choices for someone wishing to pursue a career as an exhibit designer.

1. Institutions such as Pratt or Parsons School of Design offer good courses in industrial, graphic, and commercial design.

2. Some universities can provide a liberal arts education combined with certain skill courses.

3. A candidate can attend a professional program in a field such as architecture.

Hank Grasso suggests that once your theoretical education is completed, so much more of what is still out there to study can be learned through internships and working for diverse design firms. It also gives the new exhibit designer a chance to build up a portfolio, an important tool for moving on to the next position.

Salaries

Exhibit designers work directly in museums or for private firms on contract with museums. Not surprisingly, salaries paid by the private sector often top those a museum can pay, even if the designer is doing the same work in the same institution.

Annual salaries for entry-level workers can range from $17,000 to $23,000 and are several thousand dollars higher in a private firm. An exhibit designer with over 10 years of experience could expect to earn somewhere in the $40,000s.

Notes From a Student Intern's Journal

In addition to his other duties, exhibit designer Hank Grasso is often responsible for the supervision of interns. Kendra Lambert from Auburn University in Alabama was one of his students. In 1991 she spent her last summer in college learning about graphic design at the National Museum of American History. Here are some of the notes she kept on her experiences there:

Attended staff meetings for American Encounters. Met curators, designers, educators, and the team writer along with other interns working on the project. At these meetings each team member's thoughts were expressed concerning deadlines, progress to data, and objectives. Interaction is clearly important to working as a team.

I helped build a prototype of two cases, Pueblo and Spanish missions, within the exhibit. Maps were enlarged from photocopies and mounted on foam core. Time lines were set on the Macintosh using a Pagemaker program, then cut and mounted to be used on a larger scale. The purpose of the prototype was to test audience reaction to typefaces used. Hank wanted to find out if people are sensitive to these "subtleties" in type and if symbols help some people break down information. . . . Curators also reworked some of the labels. It meant more work for the design department, but it was important to have an accurate representation of the cases.

I learned to draw objects to scale working on the Feed Bags as Fashion case. I was responsible for the title logo. Hank wanted to work from the original stencil face from an actual feed bag. It became too complex to create letterforms when we had no reference.

During Feed Bags I got to work in the Exhibit Production Lab. I helped set type for labels . . . I observed the process for silkscreening . . . I positioned the text on panels . . . It was great to be part of production! And within hours of opening the exhibit, the press was there. It was great . . . and such a huge audience response. People loved it.

I have learned that designing exhibits requires a person who is flexible to schedule the meetings that are a part of working in a team and still complete the required drawing and model work.

It is important for an exhibit designer to make an exhibit more accessible to the public so they can begin to learn what ideas the curators are attempting to communicate. . . . I have observed . . . that an exhibit designer needs a graphic artist to make decisions about type treatment, type placement, logo development and . . . creating graphics.

One of my goals this summer was to arrange portfolio reviews in the Washington, D.C. area and meet professional designers. Hank looked at my design portfolio . . . and immediately recommended I speak with a colleague. This interview taught me a lot! I also had the opportunity to meet with . . . the former director of design at the museum.

I am scheduling an appointment with the assistant of exhibition design at the National Gallery. I have recorded suggestions from these reviews that will enable me to improve my portfolio and decide on a direction for my senior project. It has been valuable also in developing interviewing skills. I feel more confident about my work and have a clearer idea of what aspect of design I will follow as a career as a result of this internship.

Kendra Lambert graduated from Auburn University in December 1991 and is currently working at the Birmingham Museum of Art as a publications designer. She designs all the printed promotional pieces that the museum uses, such as invitations, newsletters, posters, and T-shirts. She is in the process of applying to graduate school to study for a Master of Fine Arts in design history, with the ultimate goal of becoming a free-lance designer. Kendra also hopes to teach design at a university.

A Small Museum

Nauvoo, Illinois, is a historic city on the banks of the Mississippi River, near the point where Iowa, Missouri, and Illinois meet. Fairly isolated, Nauvoo is 260 miles south of Chicago and about 170 miles north of St. Louis.

Originally it had been a Sac and Fox Indian village, named Quashquema, for their chief. When Mormon founder Joseph Smith arrived in 1839, he called the site Nauvoo, from the old Hebrew word meaning "beautiful place."

The town is laid out like a mini-Williamsburg, with beautiful gardens and over two dozen restored homes and shops open to the public. Early crafts have been given a second life, and skilled artisans give daily demonstrations. Most of the staff, including the director, the guides, and caretakers, live on site. In fact, the year-round population of Nauvoo numbers only 1,100, and most of these residents work for either of the two main churches which share ownership of the town.

The Church of Jesus Christ of Latter-day Saints (the Mormons), whose headquarters is in Salt Lake City, Utah, owns and operates the Visitors Center on the north side of town as well as many other neighboring properties.

The Joseph Smith Historic Center on the south side of town is operated by the Reorganized Church of Latter-day Saints, whose headquarters is in Independence, Missouri. The Joseph Smith Historic Center has a Visitors Center which houses a greeting gallery, two theaters, and a small museum room displaying artifacts of the Smith family. There is also a library containing rare books of the period, along with reference books on the restoration and reconstruction of historic buildings and artifacts.

Visitors to the Joseph Smith Historic Center also tour the Joseph Smith Homestead whose log cabin portion was built around 1803, the 1842 Mansion House, the Smith family cemetery, and the Joseph Smith Red Brick Store, a building which was reconstructed in 1979.

Don Albro is director of historic sites at the Joseph Smith Historic Center. He feels he was chosen for this position because of his long relationship with the church (he has been an ordained minister since 1955), his interest and studies in history, and his management skills gained while in charge of an extensive sales force in private industry.

As director, Don is responsible for a full-time secretary, 2 maintenance workers, 8 student interns, and 10 senior guides who work on a volunteer basis. He coordinates the student intern program and volunteer guide staff and their training, as well as the overseeing of the historic properties and their upkeep, maintenance, and reconstruction. As director of a small museum, Don performs functions that would not normally fall under the director's realm in a larger organization. A typical day for him might also include the following tasks, which he admits are his favorites:

Conducting a tour

Assisting with cooking demonstrations at the site's Summer Kitchen

Working in the gift shop or the Red Brick Store

Repairing buildings

Trimming trees, planting flowers, weeding and cutting grass (all 34 acres of it)

Finding That Job

The *Official Museum Directory*, put out by the American Association of Museums, is a valuable resource found in the reference section of most libraries. In addition to its pages and pages of history museums and historic houses, buildings, and sites, it lists scores of historical and preservation societies, boards, agencies, councils, commissions, foundations, and research industries.

You could decide on a region where you'd like to work, then approach your choices with a phone call, resume and cover letter, or personal visit.

The American Association of Museums also puts out a monthly newsletter called *Aviso*. At least half of each issue is devoted to listings for employment opportunities and internships.

Here are just a few examples of the type of jobs advertised in one issue (because these jobs are no longer open, the employers are not identified here):

HISTORIAN II The state historical society of a northwest state is seeking a Historian II to manage the society's scholarly history magazine. Responsibilities include editing agency newsletters, developing materials for state historic sites, and providing assistance with planning the society's public programs. Minimum qualifications: M.A. in history, English, or journalism, plus proven experience in editing, design, and layout. Salary: $21,000–$33,000.

MUSEUM ARCHIVIST   A public museum in the Midwest is seeking a half-time archivist to manage its collection of materials related to local history. Minimum requirement of bachelor's degree in archives administration, U.S. history, or library science, and three years professional experience.

DIRECTOR   Director for historic house museum and garden. Seeking creative, energetic individual to oversee exciting house museum. Responsibilities include collections management, exhibit and educational program development. Background in decorative arts and ability to work with board and volunteers important.

SITE DIRECTOR Famous American author's home. All facets of historic site management including staffing, interpretation, and event planning. Museum management degree or equivalent, plus proven experience. Salary: mid- to upper $30,000s.

INTERNSHIP   A museum of archeology and anthropology at an eastern university anticipates funding for a nine-month collections management internship. Interns participate in a comprehensive training program and supervise volunteers in storage renovations and computer inventory of a designated collection. Candidate should be interested in a museum career and have a background in archeology/anthropology or museum studies. Stipend: $9,000.

Further Information

The following three reports are put out by the American Association of Museums. They may be ordered by calling or writing:

American Association of Museums
Attn: Bookstore
P.O. Box 40
Washington, DC 20042-0040
(202) 289-1818

Careers in Museums: A Variety of Vocations. Gives a broad overview of professional career opportunities in museums, suggests educational qualifications and experience for specific positions, and provides information on how to obtain internships. It also lists job placement resources.

Museum Studies Programs: Guide to Evaluation. Answers questions about the curriculum and quality of museum studies programs.

Museum Studies Programs in the United States: A Resource Guide. Provides information on training opportunities, internships and fellowships, mid-career opportunities, and management programs.

CHAPTER FIVE

Jobs for Structure Lovers

Preserving the Past

Architectural historians, architectural conservators, curators of structures, restoration architects, and other preservationists all share a love of historic buildings and architecture. They might specialize in a particular period or style, fascinated by Victorian gingerbread, strong red brick, or Federal woodwork and old frame farmhouses and barns. Most, however, are generalists, possessing knowledge that crosses the centuries. These professionals are good researchers or artists who have strong organizational skills and an interest in the environment as well as history.

The activity of preservation includes several different categories which are outlined here:

Adaptive Reuse—providing a new function for older structures that would otherwise be demolished. For example, a defunct mill is converted into an office building or a college.

Architectural Conservation—using special techniques to halt further deterioration of building materials.

Restoration (often prefaced with "Historical" or "Architectural")—involving the meticulous return of a building to its former appearance at a particular period in history.

Rehabilitation or Renovation—altering or upgrading existing buildings and structures.

Architectural Conservators

Architectural conservators are not necessarily registered architects. They might have started out in the construction and contracting field, gaining along the way specialized technical experience in problems that occur with historic buildings. Some of these problems involve the historic building fabric, such as cracks in foundations and walls, water seepage, and how to clean the building. Architectural conservators understand how buildings were constructed during earlier periods and know what kinds of complications result from the natural course of time and different climatic and environmental conditions. They are familiar with building materials, roofs, windows, exterior cladding, and various reconstruction types, such as wood-frame or masonry-clad structures.

Architectural conservators are also sometimes known as curators of structures.

Meet a Curator of Structures

A curator, in the general sense of the word, is a caregiver—someone who takes care of, for example, art collections, research documents, textiles, or historic buildings. Curators of structures work in art and history museums, living history museums, and for historical societies and associations.

Mark Fortenberry has been the curator of structures with the Nantucket Historical Association since 1987. He is responsible for the maintenance of the 12 different historic sites owned and operated by the association, and he is specifically concerned with architectural accuracy in terms of period. He also supervises contractors and technicians who are hired to perform restorations and construct reproductions. Some of the sites include the Oldest House, the Hawden House, the Thomas Macy Warehouse, and the Old Mill.

Mark talks about his duties:

When I first came to the association I was involved heavily with fieldwork—replication and carpentry. Right now, as curator of structures, I work more on an administrative level; I coordinate the restoration and repair work that goes on in the buildings. This involves meeting with architects, long range planning, scheduling, budgets. We continually upgrade each building as budget permits; we not only do routine maintenance, but more serious work in terms of maintaining the historical integrity of the building and how it is presented to the public. We are also concerned with safety to the public, security systems, providing handicap access, and environmental upgrading such as cooling and heating systems.

I also work closely with the different offices within the association. For example, we're doing a project right now refurbishing the interior of one of the house museums, so I'm coordinating with the curator of collections on that.

My job is multifaceted. Because we are a relatively small organization—16 or so full-time professionals—I have to be prepared to take on a wide range of tasks. Normally, a better-funded organization would have an architect on staff, would have someone else in charge of security, but those duties all fall under my umbrella.

Background

Mark grew up in Nantucket, a town where every building is on the National Register of Historic Places. Under those conditions, it's easy to see how his interest in history developed. Before joining the Nantucket Historical Association as a full time employee, Mark was self-employed as a restoration carpenter for over 20 years. He also worked with the Massachusetts Historic Commission and did volunteer work for the Nantucket Historic Commission, designing exhibits and constructing showcases, among other things.

He has always enjoyed working on older buildings. On the island there is a strong sensitivity toward maintaining the feeling that Nantucket is from another time. With Mark's experience and love of Nantucket, it was only natural that the Nantucket Historical Association would invite him on board as a full-time curator.

Restoration Architect

A restoration architect or an architect specializing in historic preservation has much of a general architect's experience. He or she understands how to plan spaces, how to organize construction materials, and how to put together construction documents.

The difference between a general architect and a restoration architect is that the latter's work experience has primarily been focused on historic buildings. In addition, the restoration architect will have a specialized knowledge and understanding of federal, state, and local regulations with regard to historic preservation and will also be aware of the standards set by the particular style of architecture.

Meet a Restoration Architect

Peter Benton earned a B.S. in architecture in 1972 from the University of Virginia in Charlottesville. He worked for several years for various firms in Philadelphia and Washington, D.C., then went on to complete his M. Arch. (Master's of Architecture) degree from the University of Pennsylvania in 1979.

He is now a senior associate with John Milner and Associates, Inc., a midsize architectural firm in West Chester, Pennsylvania, specializing in historic preservation. He joined the staff there in 1984 and has worked on a variety of projects.

Peter talks about his profession:

Initially I had relatively little training in preservation, but I was exposed to the idea of ecological planning at UPenn. I saw the philosophical connection between an ecological approach to the landscape and to the buildings, and that let me to historic preservation. I went to work for four or five years for an ecological planning firm, and it was there my interest developed further.

I've been responsible for all sorts of properties—anything from small, privately owned residential-scale houses from the eighteenth century to high-style nineteenth-century mansions. In addition, I've worked with historic commercial and industrial buildings from the nineteenth century, restoring them or practicing what we call adaptive reuse. For example, we recently converted an old mill into an office building and a farmhouse into a meeting facility. Another category I've worked with includes monumental buildings, such as a city hall, or large federal buildings.

The Nine Steps in a Restoration Project

1. The restoration architect first meets with the client and determines what his or her goals for the property are.

2. The restoration architect does an existing conditions analysis of the site, looks at the historical development of the building over time, and takes photographs, field measurements, and written notes.

3. Next the restoration architect does a schematic plan, making preliminary drawings and sketches, describing a design to the client for the client's approval. This stage could take four weeks or so.

4. Once the client approves the project, the restoration architect produces an outline of the scope of the work and figures an order of magnitude cost estimate.

5. After that stage is approved, the next phase is to work on design development documents. This involves the use of more detailed drawings and can take from six to eight weeks.

6. Over the next eight to twelve weeks, construction documents including drawings and specifications are produced.

7. The contractor is selected during the bidding phase.

8. Construction plans are reviewed before actually beginning work.

9. The restoration architect makes frequent visits to the site while the project is in progress. Construction time varies but could take eight months or a year and a half, depending upon the scope of the project.

Salaries

Someone fresh from graduate school can expect to earn from $25,000 to $27,000 per year, depending upon the size of the firm, the importance of the project, and the region of the country. Advancement would depend upon ability and accomplishments. An experienced architect with five years or more at the project manager level could expect to earn about $40,000 a year in a midsize firm. Those with specializations in demand can earn more.

Most firms offer paid internships for graduate students.

Architectural Historian

Architectural historians are historians with an interest in architecture. They are generally not registered architects. They often work with restoration architects, however, conducting specialized investigations and performing all the research necessary to get a restoration project underway. They dig up a building's history—when it was constructed, what its original purpose was, how long it was vacant, whether any changes had been made. They then put together a historic structures report for the architect who wants to make his or her restoration work as accurate as possible.

Architectural historians can work in academic settings, for private architectural firms, and for government agencies concerned with historic preservation.

Background

The minimum requirement for an architectural historian is an undergraduate degree in history or architectural history, although most positions require a graduate degree.

Historical Interiors Designer

To achieve complete authenticity, the interior of a historic building must be given as much attention as the exterior, especially if the building will be used as a museum open to the public.

Historic interiors designers can be architects or specially trained professionals. They must be experienced in the investigation, documentation, research, and analysis of the lighting, furnishings, finishes, and decorative arts of building interiors. Historic interiors specialists generally work as part of a team with the restoration architect and conservator.

The National Trust for Historic Preservation

The National Trust for Historic Preservation is a nonprofit organization with over 250,000 individual members. Most of the National Trust's funding comes from membership dues, corporation and foundation grants, endowment income, and merchandise sales. About 22 percent comes from a matching grant awarded by the U.S. Congress through the U.S. Department of the Interior.

The National Trust's mission is, in part, to preserve and revitalize the livability of U.S. communities by leading the nation in saving America's historic environments. It provides technical advice and financial assistance to nonprofit organizations and public agencies engaged in preservation, as well as to the general public. The National Trust also acts as an advocate for protection of the country's heritage in the courts and with legislative and regulatory agencies.

The National Trust believes that the employment outlook in the historic preservation field has grown dramatically since the early 1980s. Its concerns have enlarged from a relatively small number of historic sites, museums, and buildings to historic neighborhoods, commercial districts, and rural landscapes.

The growing sophistication of the field is reflected in the greater diversity of professionals who contribute to preservation work. Historians, curators, and other museum professionals are now joined by architects, lawyers, designers, realtors, planners, developers, mortgage lenders, and others. Once found working only in museums, libraries, and historical societies, preservationists now are also employed in real estate firms that specialize in historical properties and in financial institutions that invest in older neighborhoods.

The National Trust employs many specialists in its national office in Washington, D.C., and in its seven regional offices. In addition, the National Trust owns and operates 18 historic house museums. It also publishes *Historic Preservation* magazine and *Historic Preservation News*, which are distributed to members. The latter lists jobs opportunities and internships within both the National Trust and outside organizations.

To join (individual memberships cost $15), call or write:

National Trust for Historic Preservation
1785 Massachusetts Ave, NW
Washington, DC 20036
(202) 673-4000

Further Information

You may wish to obtain the *Guide to Graduate Degree Programs in Architectural History*, compiled by Richard Betts. It is available by contacting:

Society of Architectural Historians
1232 Pine Street
Philadelphia, PA 19107
(215) 735-0224

CHAPTER SIX

Jobs in Historical Societies
Explaining the Past

T he mission of most preservation boards and historical societies is to preserve, protect, defend, and promote the cultural, social, economic, environmental, and architectural integrity of their particular district or historic site.

Preservation boards and historical societies offer full-time employment or volunteer opportunities for most of the career categories discussed in this book. Architectural historians, archivists, restoration architects, researchers, design experts, curators, information officers, and administrators work as a team to achieve their goals.

Many boards and societies are membership-funded; others might receive government or private grants to carry on their work. The better-funded operations are able to hire specialists to work in their particular fields. Boards and societies with limited funds rely heavily on professionals willing to volunteer their time. The few paid employees take on a variety of tasks crossing career categories.

Information Officer

Although George Neary's official title is administrative director of the Miami Design Preservation League, he also functions as the sole full-time information officer for the League's Art Deco District.

George earned his B.A. degree in history at St. Anselm College in Manchester, New Hampshire, in 1970. After teaching for many years, he moved to Miami and started with the Miami Design Preservation League as a volunteer in September 1991. In March 1992 he was hired as a full-time employee.

George talks about his job with the Miami Design Preservation League:

We're a membership-funded organization, operating solely on membership dues, conducting tours, and by putting on special events throughout the year. My assistant and I are the league's only paid employees. Everyone else is a volunteer. We have over 40 volunteers which include a cadre of dedicated tour guides and office helpers. We also have the chairman and the board and various committee heads and members, all volunteer professionals.

The most important task we're focused on is the preservation of the Art Deco District. Our governmental affairs committee works with the city on zoning and other issues to protect the district from demolition or misuse. We also have an executive committee, an architectural task force, an archivist, educational committees, tour committees, special events committees, historians and writers.

Most of my time is spent in the role of information officer, working with the public. I make sure all members are kept informed of what's going on in the District. I handle huge mailings and send out press releases or call the radio stations when special shows are scheduled.

When we're putting on a major event, such as the Art Deco Weekend, I have to make sure that everything runs smoothly. I am also involved with the budgeting process, assigning tasks to staff members, and supervising tour guides. Occasionally I give a tour myself to special interest groups from out of town.

I also work as a liaison with the city, state, and federal governments. We rally the troops, lobbying to halt demolition permits, getting laws passed to protect the district.

I arrange for monthly speakers and encourage our members to attend. The members are very important to our operation. When they join the league, their dues support our activities. Members are entitled to certain privileges such as receiving the newsletter we publish, invitations to monthly gatherings and lectures, and our annual meeting, which is also open to the public.

Tour Guides and Docents

It is debatable whether there is any difference between the term
tour guide and the most common usage of the word *docent*. Although the *Random House College Dictionary* defines a docent as
"a college or university lecturer," and a privatdocent as "a lecturer
paid directly by his or her students," many consider a docent
synonymous with a tour guide.

Depending on your place of employment, a tour guide may or
may not be in costume. A tour guide is not primarily responsible
for conducting his or her own research and does not usually
portray one particular character. In addition, a tour guide doesn't
usually speak from a prepared script; a tour guide must have a
broader, more general knowledge of the area and period.

Tour guides may be employed by the federal or state government, historical societies, museums, or by a private enterprise.
They can also be self-employed.

Tour guides might ride in front of a bus or boat, microphone in
hand; be stationed in a particular building or site such as a church,
museum, or fort; share space with visitors in a horse-drawn carriage or buggy; or lead visitors around on foot on historical walking
tours.

Meet a Tour Guide in Miami Beach's
Art Deco District

Most people think of Miami Beach as the place everyone's grandmother lives. For a long time, Collins Avenue and Ocean Drive,
packed with residential hotels and condominiums, did cater to the
over-60 set. But in the last 15 years the demographics, as well as
the topography, have been changing.

Jeff Donnelly is a volunteer tour guide for the Miami Design
Preservation League. He knows the area as well as anyone. Mon-
day through Friday he teaches history and political science at a
local day school in Dade County. And for the past five years on
Saturday mornings, he's been donning his Panama hat and walk-

ing shoes and taking groups on 90-minute strolling tours through Miami Beach's newly restored Art Deco District.

"Miami Beach is an exciting place to live these days," Jeff explains. "Young professionals, artists, models, movie production people—they're all flocking here now. We've become very chic."

After cautioning the 20 or so in his group—from New York, Texas, Colorado, and nearby Fort Lauderdale—about the strong Florida sun ("If anyone feels dehydrated, please raise your hand before you pass out"), he provides them with more than just a passing glimpse into Miami's new mystique.

"As elderly residents moved into nursing homes or passed away, investors and developers began buying up and renovating the run-down buildings," he says. "In the process, they uncovered the fantasy seaside resort that had first inspired the original boom back in the 1920s and '30s.

"There were five major architects responsible for the district. Although they were commercial competitors, they were also coffee-klatch friends. If someone's building supplies hadn't arrived on time or if someone ran short, they lent materials back and forth. This, of course, explains the high level of style consistency throughout the district."

The old establishments, once painted white and trimmed with only powder blue, aquamarine, or the peaches and pinks of aging flamingos, have now received fresh face-lifts and glow with a contemporary pastel palette. Bands of lavender, blue, yellow, aqua and a whole spectrum of pinks whimsically decorate oceanfront hotels, sidewalk cafes, model agencies, and apartment buildings.

Miami Beach can boast of the largest concentration of Art Deco buildings in the country; over 800 contribute to the historic or architectural nature of the Art Deco District. The result is a Disneyesque urban streetscape, as fanciful as Victorian gingerbread, with the promise of campy humor and fun.

"You'd almost expect to see flappers strolling arm in arm or Al Capone roaring up in his jalopy," observed one member of the tour group. In fact, it's rumored that Al Capone often ate at the Park Central, one of the hotels along Ocean Drive, with his bodyguards perched on the overhead balcony for protection. Whether that story is true or not, the gangster movie *Scarface* was filmed there.

The term *art deco,* meaning a bold and linear form of art combining art moderne, cubism, futurism, and expressionism, wasn't coined until the 1960s, but it refers to the style that became popular in the 1920s and 1930s, originating in Paris. In its day, Miami Beach's architecture was considered ultramodern; the goal was to be futuristic, to look ahead. In the grip of the Great Depression, the architects and designers wanted to convey the message that happy days were coming.

But the Art Deco area is not a historic district which seeks to preserve exactly what was there in the twenties and thirties.

"We're not a Williamsburg," says Jeff. "Our philosophy is what we call 'adaptive reuse'—restoration projects focus on designs with contemporary uses. It allows for a larger variety of colors and for more of the surface areas to be given over to color."

Anyone who wants to renovate must bring their plans to the Miami Preservation League Review Board for approval. "The Tuesday night meetings are a great source of local entertainment," says Jeff. "The number of arguments presented over color choices are fascinating."

The Miami Design Preservation League was established in 1976 and is the oldest Art Deco organization in the world. For three years they cataloged the Art Deco and Mediterranean Revival–style buildings, earning a listing in the National Register of Historic Places. The league's main function now is to guard against demolitions, incompatible construction and false restorations.

"We don't want new construction to completely imitate the old style," Donnelly says. "There's a Kentucky Fried Chicken that slipped by before the review board was established. It looks so much like a building from the twenties—it confuses people."

But the hotels that line Ocean Drive are the real thing. Many are named after posh New York establishments to convey a sense of luxury—the Ritz, the Waldorf Towers; some are named after the designers' family members—the Victor, the Adrian.

It's not only the bright colors that attract the eye. Special attention to form, detail, and vertical and horizontal lines makes up the art deco style. Buildings have varying themes: streamline moderne rounded corners accented with "eyebrows," sky-pointing needlelike finials (the Breakwater Hotel's allegedly were used in an early Buck Rogers film), rare etched-glass windows, fluted cornices, stepped rooflines, horizontal racing stripes, and nautical moderne porthole windows.

The Avalon hotel has added a special touch to complete the pretty picture—a 1950 shiny chrome and yellow-and-white Oldsmobile is regularly parked in front of the yellow-painted building. Quite a number of advertising and modeling agencies use the hotel for a backdrop on photographic shoots.

Indeed, any morning of the week, when the early eastern light splashes across the soft colors, five or six different shoots are usually in progress. "Miami Vice" TV show scenes were frequently shot along Ocean Drive, and more and more celebrities visit the area.

Regular special events add even more life to this spirited district. One of those events is the Art Deco Weekend, held annually on the second weekend of January. It relives the days of the Big Band, speakeasies, and street theater against Miami Beach's classic art deco backdrop. Antique cars, period artwork, collectibles and memorabilia carry visitors back to the Roaring Twenties.

Nighttime brings a new dimension to the Art Deco District. Neon tube lighting was first invented in the late 1930s, and Ocean Drive was a showcase for this exciting new discovery.

"It must have been a magical experience for those seeing the glowing colorful lights against the glass block for the first time," says Jeff.

Many of the lobbies inside the hotels are equally magical. Original murals and paintings of the era decorate the walls, and colorful terrazzo stone chips cover the floors in geometric patterns.

Jeff points out the last stop, the Blackstone Hotel, where George Gershwin reputedly wrote "Porgy and Bess," then steers his group back to the Art Deco Welcome Center.

"It's ironic, really," Jeff concludes. "We've put a lot of effort into preserving an era which actually stood for forward movement, growth, and development. But the architects of the time hit on just the right note for Miami Beach. What was beautiful then is even more beautiful now. It's certainly worth preserving."

For more information on the Art Deco District, contact:

Miami Design Preservation League
P.O. Box Bin L
Miami Beach, FL 33119
(305) 672-2014.

Meet a Docent for the Nantucket Historical Association

Jeremy Slavitz is a paid docent for the Nantucket Historical Association. Although he grew up in a location noted for its historical significance, it wasn't until he attended college that his interest in history developed. He wasn't sure what he wanted to do, so he enrolled in a variety of classes. The history courses interested him the most, and he discovered it was important to work in a discipline he enjoyed. He graduated from the University of Massachusetts, Amherst, in 1992 with a bachelor's degree in history, specializing in naval history. He plans to go on to complete a graduate degree. The summer of 1992 was his first season as a docent.

Jeremy talks about his job:

What I like most about working for the Historical Association is that it gives me a chance to work in history, but I'm not stuck in a closet doing research. I can get out and talk to people. Docenting has helped me to realize I might enjoy a career in teaching history. I'm giving information every day, struggling to make it interesting for them. I enjoy the challenge.

The docents always work in pairs, and that's one of the other aspects that helps to make the job fun. There are several other college students employed as well as the older residents. We alternate taking guests through. On a rainy day, we're very busy, with not much time to rest. When the sun is out, most visitors to Nantucket head for the beach. Then the day goes a bit slower.

The docents with the Historical Association try to portray our museums throughout their history. Rather than just identifying a certain object, a chair or a table, we try to give visitors a more three-dimensional picture of the people who were living there through various time periods, and the different ways the building was used.

For example, one of the properties I work in is Nantucket's Oldest House. It was built in 1686 by Jethro Coffin. He was a wealthy businessman, and at that time his house was one of the largest on the island and was considered the most prestigious. We show the house as it was then, and we show it as it was during the eighteenth century after another owner, Nathaniel Paddock, bought it. He was a weaver and he worked on his loom in the home. During his time, as the island population grew, the house was considered to be of modest proportions and no longer held the same prestige. We also show the house as it is now, a small structure with three rooms on the ground floor and two rooms upstairs.

I don't work from a prepared script. We do have a general guideline to follow, but I have the freedom to tailor my presentation based on who is visiting. Last summer there was a local boy whose parents were members of the historical association. They gave him their pass, which allows admission to about 12 different properties, put him on his bicycle and sent him on his way. He would bring his friends, and over the course of the summer he followed me around to the different sites where I worked. He'd wait until most of the other visitors had left, so I could show him parts of the buildings he would find the most interesting. They peered up chimneys and climbed through root cellars and figured out how the loom worked. They had a great time. Someone else would have an entirely different interest, so I would focus on another aspect for them.

How Nantucket Historical Association Docents are Trained

Jeremy explains:

The training process was very enjoyable. In each museum there is a book that has been put together which includes all the known information about the house or building. On top of that, there are people here who have done this for years, so a lot of the training has to do with oral history. We're learning from people who have learned from people before them. Some of the older docents have lived on the island all of their lives and they can pass down the history, as well as their own experiences with the property.

Hours and Salary

Jeremy puts in as many hours as possible and generally works a 40-hour week spread over six days. Because one of the museums is open at night, he also is on duty for some evening hours.

He is paid $6 an hour. Although the salary is low, and the only benefits are, as he puts it, "I have a job," Jeremy is happy with his work.

Further Information

Confessions of a Tour Leader, by Baxter and Corinne Geeting, offers a witty and sophisticated look at the real-life experiences of a college faculty couple who became summertime tour leaders. The publisher is Prima Publishing.

CHAPTER SEVEN

Jobs for Diggers
Uncovering the Past

M ost history professionals are diggers, both literally and
figuratively—they dig up information from the past.
Some dig through mounds of dirt for relics and other
evidence of past civilizations and cultures; others seek facts digging through mounds of paper.

Archeologist

Archeology is a subdivision of the field of anthropology.
Archeologists study the artifacts of past cultures to learn about
their history, customs, and living habits. They survey and exca-
vate archeological sites, recording and cataloging their finds. By
careful analysis, archeologists reconstruct earlier cultures and
determine their influence on the present.

Archeological sites are the physical remains of past civilizations. They can include building debris and the items found
inside, in addition to trash and garbage. Usually these sites have
been buried by other, later human activity or by natural processes.

Excavation of these sites is a painstaking process conducted by
professionals using modern techniques. Because these sites are so
fragile, the very nature of excavating destroys some information.
With this in mind, archeologists are careful to dig only as much

as they need to answer important questions. Frequently, archeologists concentrate their work on sites slated for destruction to make room for highway or new building construction.

Archeologists work in a variety of settings. The following chart lists these settings and the duties specific to each.

SETTING	DUTIES	WORKING CONDITIONS
Universities and Colleges, Private Institutions	Teaching, Field Work, Research, Directing Student Field Work	Classroom, Labs, Office Space
Museums	Field Work, Research, Classifying, Preserving, Displaying	Display and Research Areas, Office Space
Public Sector (local, state, and national government agencies)	Excavating, Surveying Analyzing Preserving and Recording Remains	On Site, Labs, Research Facilities
Private Sector (construction companies, architectural firms)	Excavating, Surveying Preserving and Recording Remains	On Site, Labs, Research Facilities

Archeologists conducting field work often work with several other professionals in a team effort. They are assisted by geologists, ethnologists, educators, anthropologists, ecologists, and aerial photographers.

In the field, archeologists use a variety of tools during an excavation. These include picks, shovels, trowels, wheelbarrows, sifting boxes, pressure sprayers, and brushes. Archeologists also make drawings and sketches on site and take notes and photographs.

What It Takes to Become an Archeologist

Do you have what it takes to become an archeologist? Take this Self-Evaluation Quiz and find out.

Put a check mark under the appropriate heading.　　YES　NO

1. I have above-average academic ability. ____ ____

2. I have an avid interest in science and history. ____ ____

3. Hours of strenuous activity (lifting, carrying, shoveling) do not pose a problem for me.

4. I have been told I have leadership qualities. ____ ____

5. The idea of continuing study throughout my career appeals to me. ____ ____

6. I am a logical and analytical thinker. ____ ____

7. I enjoy working independently. ____ ____

8. I function well as part of a team. ____ ____

9. I believe professional ethics should be strictly adhered to. ____ ____

10. I can live under primitive conditions in remote areas. ____ ____

To consider yourself a potential archeologist, you must have been able to check YES for every question. Even with just one NO, you might want to reconsider your choice of field. Archeology is an extremely rigorous and competitive profession.

Background

To qualify as a professional archeologist, graduate study leading to a master's degree is necessary. A doctoral degree is often preferable. Most graduate programs in archeology are found in anthropology departments. There are about 30 universities maintaining schools of archeology; these are listed in the *Peterson's Guide to Graduate and Professional Programs*. To gain the necessary background at the undergraduate level, a study of anthropology, history, art, geology, or a related field should be pursued. At the graduate level, students following a course in archeology would also have to include cultural and physical anthropology and linguistics in their curriculum.

Job Opportunities

Relatively few openings exist in the field of teaching archeology. Recently, however, more federal grants and contracts have been made available for archeological field work and research. A lot of this work is being conducted in the western and southwestern states, such as Colorado, Arizona, and New Mexico. Particularly in northwestern New Mexico, there is a strong industry developing resources such as gas and oil. Because much of the land there is owned by the Federal Bureau of Land Management, professional archeologists must be hired to clear the site before gas lines or wells can be put in.

In addition to that, the building of a reservoir on the Dolores River in Colorado uncovered hundreds of archeological sites, necessitating a great deal of archeological work. The project, which is the largest on the continent and has a very attractive budget, has since brought many archeologists to that area.

Interested history buffs who do not desire a full-time professional career as an archeologist, but would like to experience archeological work, can find many opportunities to try their hands at a dig. If you are willing to invest your time—and in some cases, your money—you can easily find professionally supervised archeological investigations taking on volunteers. These are listed in *Archeology* magazine or in the books mentioned at the end of this section. A few other examples of places to contact are provided here:

Crow Canyon
  Archeological Center
23390 County Road K
Cortez, CO 81321
(800) 422-8975

Earthwatch
680 Mt. Auburn Street
Box 403N
Watertown, MA 02272
(617) 926-8200

University Research
Expeditions Program
Department J-4
University of California
Berkeley, CA 94720
(415) 642-6586

Center for American Archeology
Department B
Kampsville Archeological Center
P.O. Box 366
Kampsville, IL 62053
(618) 653-4316

Foundations for
  Field Research
P.O. Box 2010
Alpine, CA 91001
(619) 445-9264

The Smithsonian Institution
Smithsonian National Associates
Research Expedition Program
490 L'Enfant Plaza, SW,
  Suite 4210
Washington, DC 20560
(202) 357-1350

Close-up: Crow Canyon Archeological Center

Crow Canyon is a nonprofit research and educational institution funded by tuition fees, donations, and federal grants. It features an 80-acre campus in southwestern Colorado, near Mesa Verde National Park, with a staff of about 50 archeologists, educators, and support staff. In addition to its own research, the institution instructs participants, both adults and children, who want to learn about archeology. From junior high age on, participants are taken into the field and taught excavation, recording, and documentation techniques. They also work in the lab a few days a week learning analysis techniques and methods for cleaning artifacts.

Children too young to work in the field can still participate in a simulated dig in a lab Crow Canyon has set up for that purpose. There they can learn the same excavating techniques as they sift through large, shallow sandboxes where artifacts and walls and other features are buried, just as they would be in the field.

Participants come from all over the United States on educational vacations and stay for a three-to-five-day program. Crow Canyon also works with about a dozen graduate students of archeology a year, providing rewarding internships.

During the summer months, participants sleep in cabin tents or hogans, circular Navaho-style structures.

In Montezuma County, where Crow Canyon is located, there are over 100,000 archeological sites. Crow Canyon professionals at two different nearby sites—Sand Canyon Pueblo and Castle Rock Pueblo, both on Bureau of Land Management land. The sites were once Anasazi Indian villages. The Anasazi are the ancestors of present-day Pueblo Indians and were in this area of Colorado from the sixth century until about the year 1300. When they vacated the area, they headed for various points south and relocated. The Crow Canyon team's research is focusing on when exactly the Anasazi left and why. They are also investigating the political and social systems of the Anasazi.

Kristin Kuckelman is a field anthropologist at Crow Canyon Archaeologist Center. Her interest began when she was a child. Kristin's father was in the U.S. Air Force, and she traveled with her parents around the world. They were interested in different cultures and in archeology as well and passed that interest on to their daughter. When it came time to go to college, Kristin was naturally drawn to the anthropology program.

Kristin talks about her job:

I love the variety of it, I enjoy working outdoors, I enjoy writing. And with any kind of research, there's the excitement of discovery. You're trying to solve problems, you're trying to find things out, you're trying to learn something new. And basically, every time you go in the field you hope you're going to learn something about a culture that no one knew before. You don't know what that's going to be; you never really know how it's going to turn out or what you're going to find.

The sites in this particular area are very easy to discern. They have many hundreds of masonry rooms with, even after centuries, telltale piles of rubble and thousands of artifacts scattered about the ground. Just from walking around the modern ground surface, you can see the tops of the walls and the depressions in the ground indicating the subterranean chambers.

Sand Canyon covers about 4 acres. Castle Rock is smaller, close to 3 acres, and is situated around the base of a butte, a small flat-topped mountain.

Because of the subterranean chambers, we sometimes have to dig down to $2\frac{1}{2}$ to 3 meters to find the actual floor of the structure. The surface rooms are shallower, but we can still have a meter, a meter and a half filled in.

We've found lithic artifacts, which are artifacts made out of stone, such as spear and arrow points, and sandstone tools for grinding grain. We've also found tens of thousands of pottery fragments—very rarely do we find a piece that is still intact. And very rarely do we engage in refitting, trying to piece the shards together. With so many pieces scattered over the ground, it would take many years, be very, very expensive, and would certainly drive someone crazy!

Beginning with the first week in May, which is the start of our field season, my partner and I head out to the site, set up equipment, and make sure we have the areas we want excavated all laid out and prepared. We take care of all our paperwork and any mapping we have to do so we're ready for participants to begin digging.

During the digging season we take participants out 2 or 3 days a week, but the first full day is spent on campus. Our educators give them a full orientation about archeology in general. Out in the field, we give them a site tour to give them a background on what it is we're going to be digging, why we're digging, what we're trying to learn. We then give them tools and individual instruction, and place them, either individually or in pairs, at the particular places we want excavated.

Basically we move dirt and put it in a bucket and then take it to a screening station, which is a quarter-inch mesh screen. The dirt gets sifted through the screen to make sure we're not losing any artifacts. Everybody has their own bag to keep artifacts from each excavation area separate.

Near the end of the season we have quite a bit of documentation and mapping to do, and we wash and analyze the artifacts. When we're finished with them, most of the artifacts are put in storage, though a few are rotated as exhibits at the Anasazi Heritage Center, a federally run curation facility.

Then we have to fill the areas we've dug back in with all the screened dirt and rocks we originally dug out. The idea is if you were to walk across the site a year later, you'd never know there had been an excavation there. For safety reasons, we can't leave gaping holes in the land, and in terms of conservation, to leave a pit open to the elements would damage the site.

Before we close it back up, we line the pit with landscaping fabric to protect it, and to provide a clue in case future archeologists are digging there but do not have access to our notes and maps. The lining would show them the site had already been excavated. There are so many sites, and to keep a site open and developed for public exhibit, as has been done at Mesa Verde, would be extremely expensive. It would also be very hard on the architecture itself. Constant maintenance would have to be performed or everything would eventually deteriorate.

During the winter we write up in report form everything we learned the previous summer. We also write articles for professional journals and present papers at archeological conferences across the country.

Background

Kristin graduated in 1975 with a B.A. in anthropology and psychology from Colorado Women's College (which has now merged with the University of Denver), and earned her master's degree in anthropology with a concentration in archeology from the University of Texas, Austin, in 1977.

Further Reading

Archaeological Fieldwork Opportunities Bulletin, compiled by the Archaeological Institute of America. Can be ordered through Kendall Hunt Publishing Company, Order Dept, 2640 Kerper Boulevard, Dubuque, IA 52001, 1-800-338-5578. It is a comprehensive guide to excavations, field schools, and special programs throughout the world with openings for volunteers, students, staff, and technicians.

Summer Field School List, American Anthropological Association, 1703 New Hampshire Avenue, NW, Washington, DC 20009, (202) 232-8800.

LEAP: Listing of Education in Archeological Programs, available from LEAP coordinator, DCA/ADD, National Park Service, P.O. Box 37127, Washington, DC 20013-7127

Books

America's Ancient Treasures, by Franklin and Mary Elting, University of New Mexico Press.

Archeology: Theories, Methods, and Practice, by Colin Renfrew and Paul Bahn, Thames and Hudson, New York.

The Adventure of Archeology, by Brian M. Fagan, National Geographic Society, Washington, D.C.

Magazines

Archaeology, Bimonthly published by the Archaeological Institute of America.
National Geographic, Monthly.
Scientific American, Monthly.
Smithsonian, Monthly.

Professional Journals

These journals, though not available in every local library, can be found in university libraries or in large public libraries.

American Antiquity
Historical Archaeology
Journal of Anthropological Archaeology
Journal of Field Archaeology
North American Archaeologist

Archivist

Nobody knows the exact number, but it's estimated that there are close to 5,000 archives in the United States. Each of the 50 states maintains government archives, as do most city and county governments. Archives will also be found in universities, historical societies, museums, libraries, and private businesses.

On the national level, there is the National Archives in Washington, D.C., which looks after the records of the federal government. The Library of Congress provides information services to the U.S. Congress and technical services to all the libraries across the country.

Although archives are similar to libraries, there are distinct differences between the two. Libraries typically house materials that are published and were created with the express purpose of broad dissemination. Archives typically hold materials that were created in the course of carrying out some sort of business or activity, but were never intended originally for public dissemination. For example, in an archive you might find letters from a Civil

War soldier to his family. He wrote about his experiences and feelings and to let his loved ones know that he was still alive, surviving this or that battle. He never would have imagined that his correspondence would be saved for public viewing. This gives his letters credibility, an integrity as a historical source. The newspaper reporter covering the same battles is writing with a specific point of view for widespread publication, ultimately with the intention of selling newspapers.

Archives handle collections that chart the course of daily life for individuals and businesses. Some archives specifically look after materials created by their own institution. Coca-Cola Co., for example, set up an archive years ago to have a history of what the company business was and how it prospered. New companies set up archives to keep a documented record.

Other institutions, such as universities or museums, create archives that relate to their special research interests.

The material found in archives can be letters, personal papers, organizational records, and other documents. Archives created within the past 100 years or so could also contain visual records such as photographs and postcards, prints, drawings, and sketches.

Today, archives also collect recording tapes, phonograph records, movie films, videotapes, and computer-stored information.

Because archives hold firsthand information, they are valuable to anyone with an interest in the people, places, and events of the past. This group includes genealogists, museum researchers, scholars and students, writers, and historians.

As with libraries and archives, there are distinct differences between librarians and archivists in the way they operate and the methods and techniques they use to handle material.

The biggest single difference is that librarians look at materials they get on an item-by-item basis. Each book is a distinct entity evaluated separately from the other books. In an archive, a single letter would usually be part of a larger collection of letters. Archivists are interested in these as a group, because one letter would only be a fragment. To really understand something about the past, the information needs to be synthesized and put together from a collection.

Archivists provide a service to society by identifying and preserving materials with lasting value for the future. When archivists talk about their work, they discuss certain basic functions that are common to all archives. The numbers to the right of the following five areas designate the percentage of time usually spent on each duty.

1. Identification and acquisition of materials   10%

2. Arrangement and description of collections   60%

3. Preservation of collections   10%

4. Reference services   15%

5. Community outreach and public affairs   5%

Meet the Chief Archivist at the Smithsonian Institution's National Museum of American History

John Fleckner came to the Smithsonian in 1982 with more than a decade's experience working as an archivist for the State Historical Society of Wisconsin. He is a past president of the Society of American Archivists and has acted as a consultant on many important archives projects, including the United Negro College Fund, the Viet Nam History and Archives Project, and the Native American Archives Project.

John did his undergraduate work at Colgate, in Hamilton, New York, graduating in 1963 with a B.A. with honors in history. He earned his master's degree in American history at the University of Wisconsin in 1965. He has also amassed significant work towards a Ph.D.

The archives John is responsible for acquire collections from the outside and do not handle the records generated by the museum. Their collections cover a wide range of subjects and are particularly strong in the areas of American music, advertising, and the history of technology.

At the Smithsonian, John oversees a professional staff of 12 archivists, 3 student interns, and close to 20 volunteers. He divides his time as follows:

1. Identification and acquisition of materials   15%

2. Supervision   50%

3. Reference services   10%

4. Administration, meetings, budget, personnel   15%

5. Outreach and public affairs   10%

John talks about how he became an archivist:

After too many years of graduate school, pursuing a vague notion of teaching college-level history, I realized that I really didn't want to teach. I was so naive, it took a university career counselor to recognize that my history background might be anything other than an economic liability. Leaning back in her chair, she pointed out her office window to the State Historical Society of Wisconsin just across the street, and she directed me to a recently established graduate program in archives administration. The instructor would make no promises about the prospects for a job, but with a sly smile he offered that all his previous students were working. I didn't need a weatherman—as they said in those days, the early 1970s—to tell me which way the wind was blowing.

So, it was an accident in good guidance that got me in the door. But it was the experience of doing archival work—beginning with the simplest class exercises and then a formal internship—that sealed it for me. I loved the combination of handicraft and analytical work and I loved the intense, intimate contact with the "stuff" of history. Before I completed my internship, I knew I wanted to be an archivist.

Previously, as a graduate student, of course I had done some research in archives—at the Library of Congress, the College of William and Mary, and especially the State Historical Society. But the archivists had taken all the fun out of it. The materials were antiseptically foldered, boxed, and listed. Wheeled out on carts, they were like cadavers to be dissected by first-year medical students. On occasion I even donned white gloves. The documents always seemed lifeless.

Later, as a would-be archivist, they thrilled me. I was in charge, I would evaluate their significance, determine their order, describe their contents, and physically prepare them for their permanent resting places.

Still, it was not so much this heady feeling of control that awed me but more the mystery, the possibilities of the records themselves. My judgments would be critical to building paths to the records for generations of researchers, across the entire spectrum of topics, and into unknown future time.

The archival enterprise held another attractive feature for me. For all the opportunity to reconstruct the past captured in these documents, and to imagine the future research they might support, I had a well-defined task to accomplish, a product to produce, techniques and methods for proceeding, and standards against which my work would be judged. There was rigor and discipline; this was real work. And, as good fortune would have it, I soon was getting paid to do it.

Background

People get into the archives profession in a variety of traditional and unusual ways. Often in a small town, an archive is a closet in the back room of a local historical society's office. Someone volunteers to put it all together, perhaps the oldest person in the community with a strong interest in the area's history.

The standard way to become an archivist is to have an undergraduate degree with a history background and a graduate degree at least at the master's level that would involve specific course work in archives. There are 30 to 50 programs (the Society of American Archivists publishes a directory of these educational programs) which are often in graduate library schools.

Many archivists have a Master of Library Science (MLS) degree with a concentration in archives, but sometimes archives courses are taught in history departments.

Salaries

Archivists with a master's degree can expect to start out with an annual salary in the $24,000 to $29,000 range. Someone with 10 years of experience working as an archivist with administrative responsibilities for the Smithsonian might earn $60,000 a year or more.

Genealogist

The study of genealogy, tracing family histories, has recently become one of the most popular hobbies in the United States. Many genealogy hobbyists take their interest one step beyond tracing their own family's history and become self-employed genealogists, helping others to dig up their family trees. Genealogists also are employed in historical societies and libraries with special genealogy rooms.

The Church of Jesus Christ of Latter-day Saints in Salt Lake City, for example, has a huge repository of family information in a subterranean library. The Mormons employ genealogists all over the world, or include genealogists who have been accredited through their own program on a list of free-lance researchers. For more information, write or call:

Accreditation Program
Family History Library
35 N West Temple Street
Salt Lake City, UT 84150
(800) 453-3860

Other genealogists find work teaching their skills to others in adult education classes, by editing genealogy magazines, or by writing books or newspaper genealogy columns.

Most genealogists are not formally trained, though specializing in genealogy is possible through some university history and library science programs. In addition, a genealogist can become board-certified. For information on certification requirements and procedures write to:

Board for Certification of Genealogists
P.O. Box 5816
Falmouth, VA 22403-5816

Salaries

Salaries vary depending upon the institution where a genealogist is employed and upon the level of expertise he or she has reached. Self-employed genealogists make anywhere from $15 to $35 an hour.

How to Get Started

The National Genealogy Society makes the following suggestions for beginners:

QUESTION OLDER FAMILY MEMBERS. Encourage them to talk about their childhoods and relatives and listen carefully for clues they might inadvertently drop. Learn good interviewing techniques so you ask questions that elicit the most productive answers. Use a tape recorder and try to verify each fact through a separate source.

VISIT YOUR LOCAL LIBRARY. Become familiar with historical and genealogical publications (a few sources are provided at the end of this chapter and in Appendix D) and contact local historical societies and the state library and archives in your state capital. Seek out any specialty ethnic or religious libraries and visit cemeteries.

VISIT COURTHOUSES. Cultivate friendships with busy court clerks. Ask to see source records such as wills, deeds, marriage books, and birth and death certificates.

ENTER INTO CORRESPONDENCE. Write to other individuals or societies involved with the same families or regions. Contact foreign embassies in Washington, D.C. Restrict yourself to asking only one question in each letter you send. Include the information you have already uncovered. Include a self-addressed, stamped envelope to encourage replies.

BECOME COMPUTER LITERATE. Members of the National Genealogical Society can participate in a special computer interest section. It encourages the use of computers in research, record management, and data sharing.

KEEP PAINSTAKING RECORDS. Use printed family group sheets or pedigree charts. Develop a well-organized filing system so you'll be able to easily find your information. Keep separate records for each family you research.

WRITE TO THE NATIONAL GENEALOGICAL SOCIETY. Take advantage of its 46-page book, *Beginners in Genealogy*, its charts, and its library loan program. You can also enroll in a home-study course called American Genealogy: A Basic Course.

CHAPTER EIGHT

Some Creative Ideas
Documenting the Past

M any innovative people have combined a love of history with other talents or acquired skills. With a good imagination and a lot of drive and persistence, a dedicated history buff can bring in extra income or create a specialized career.

Here are a few successful ventures that might spark some ideas of your own.

Writing

Desktop Publishing

Prudy Taylor Board, a published author, creative writing instructor, and staff writer for her local newspaper, has established a sideline called Prudy's Press. She researches and self-publishes pamphlets covering the historic sites in her hometown of Fort Myers on the west coast of Florida. Some of her topics include Sanibel Island's famous lighthouse, the Burroughs Home, which is on the National Register of Historic Places, and an account of the history of Fort Myers.

Prudy talks about her enterprises:

In 1990 I attended a national convention for writers in San Antonio, and while I was there I paid a visit to the Alamo. They had a little booklet on sale for $1.95, a short writeup of the fort's history. I knew from all my years in Fort Myers that there was no inexpensive tourist information available there. I had a file cabinet full of information at home, and I realized I could do the same for attractions in my own area. And that's how Prudy's Press was born.

Being an active member of both the Southwest Florida Historical Society and the Fort Myers Historical Museum has helped me when it comes time to do my research. The two organizations have opened their archives to me. I also talk to the old-timers in the neighborhood and regularly visit the public library where all the past issues of newspapers dating back to 1894 are on microfilm.

When I start a book project, I run a little ad in the paper asking for information, or I generate a press release announcing the new book. I ask people to share their memories and photographs with me.

After I'm finished writing, I do the layout on my computer using a desktop publishing package. Then I take the camera-ready copy to my local printer and pay him for the printing, paper, folding, collating, and stapling. My cost runs between 50 and 75 cents per copy.

I sell the booklets at a wholesale price of $1.50 per copy to bookstores, museum and other tourist attraction gift shops. Or, I acquire a mailing list of selected markets and send out samples. I generally sell between 50 to 100 booklets a month.

I've also been contacted by various organizations to write pamphlets and booklets for them on topics of their own choosing, for which I am paid a set rate. And, in addition to a booklet and map I put together for an historic walking tour enterprise, I've co-authored three full-length books published by Donning: A *Pictorial History of Lee County*, *Pages from the Past*, and *Historic Fort Myers*.

Prudy also gives talks on local history to different civic organizations and clubs and or acts as a tour guide for an occasional historic cruise or bus tour. Her fee ranges from free, with the opportunity to sell her booklets, to a fee of $200.

Newspaper Columns

Cookie O'Brien, a long time resident of St. Augustine, Florida, and information officer for the city's preservation board, has also started a sideline. She writes a frequent column for her local newspaper, delving into the private lives of historic figures from her region. In true soap-opera fashion, which fascinates her readers, she reports the loves and scandals, adventures and tragedies that surrounded early St. Augustine inhabitants.

How to Get Started

Writers can duplicate both Prudy's and Cookie's efforts, disseminating local historic tidbits and covering characters and events from their own regions. After a trip to the public library, try writing a few sample booklets or columns, then approach museum gift shops, bookstores, civic groups, or your local editor with a query letter, phone call, or visit.

Historical Novels

On a larger scale, requiring higher degrees of skill and perseverance, writers have been entertaining readers throughout the years with epic forays into fictionalized history.

Imaginary characters are interwoven with real events and places; romance, pathos, and mystery often play a large part in the action. The author's research skills and attention to authentic detail (among other things) are what can make or break a potential sale to a publisher. Our hero can't be posing for photographs before the camera was invented or wearing a style of clothing that didn't come into fashion for 50 years.

Some successful authors in the genre are Norah Lofts and Victoria Holt.

Coffeetable Books

Coffeetable books are so named because they are handsomely designed volumes intended to be kept on display, rather than tucked away on a bookshelf. They usually focus on a particular topic and are illustrated by beautiful color photographs.

Close-up: Painted Ladies

Michael Larsen and Elizabeth Pomada, successful literary agents and authors, moved from New York and set up shop in San Francisco in the early 1970s. While their agency was still in its infancy, Michael took a part-time job as a taxi driver—and got a chance to explore their adopted city in depth. In the process, he discovered a rich treasure of American craftwork: fanciful Victorian houses. His reaction was typical of any savvy literary agent and history lover.

"Seeing those glorious houses bathed in golden California light—I knew there had to be a book in it," Michael explains.

So far, there have been six books in it. The series documents Victorians in San Francisco and across the country.

The term *Painted Lady,* now used generically to describe a multicolored Victorian home, was coined by Michael and Elizabeth in their first book *Painted Ladies: San Francisco's Resplendent Victorians.* The phrase has gone a long way toward saving Victorian homes from the wrecking ball.

"Houses of historic value, often in neighborhoods that had seen better days, were being torn down all across America," Elizabeth explains. "Someone needed to call attention to the problem—to tell people that these homes often qualified for federal loans, and that they could be given a face-lift with a new coat of paint."

The use of contrasting colors brings out the ruffles, flourishes, and other fairy-tale features common to Victorian homes, but that have been hidden under years of neglect and layers of white paint. Typical Victorian colors encompass a polychrome rainbow and include raspberry, plum, rose, grape, clay pink, pewter, lime green, and gold.

The authors write in their introduction, "Because of their beauty, craftsmanship, inexhaustible variety, the quality of materials that went into them, and their sheer numbers, Victorians are the greatest gift of America's architectural heritage."

Painted Ladies: San Francisco's Resplendent Victorians sparked what is now thought of as a color revolution. Since 1978, when the book was published, this colorist movement has spread from San Francisco to cities throughout the country.

The book has become the mainstay for the network of Victorian homeowners, preservationists, historians, architects, craftspeople, city planners, and magazine publishers. It also prompted a surge in revitalizing Victorian homes throughout America. The second book of the series, *Daughters of Painted Ladies*, covers this new generation of Painted Ladies in six regions. It instructs homeowners how to create their own Painted Lady, offers suggestions for saving derelict Victorian structures and lists valuable resources such as national preservation organizations, books, magazines, color consultants, and suppliers.

The sixth in the series, *America's Painted Ladies*, is a tribute to history, color, and architecture. The duo have also co-authored another book; this one is about Artistic License, a San Francisco Bay area guild that is revitalizing Victorian crafts.

Both Michael Larsen and Elizabeth Pomada are extremely proud of their role in preserving an important face of America's architectural heritage.

Photography

Many writers team up with photographers, as Michael Larsen and Elizabeth Pomada did for several of their *Painted Ladies* books. But a photographer with writing and/or marketing skills—and a focused project—can set out on his or her own to capture America's heritage.

In addition to colorful Victorian houses, the intricate iron balconies in New Orleans' French Quarter and the stately doors and townhouses of historic Boston have all been preserved by cameras. The resulting photographs have been reproduced as postcards, posters, greeting cards, calendars, and coffeetable books.

Here are a few other suggestions; by exploring your own neighborhood or traveling through the country, you can add to the list.

Historic forts

Early trains

Old sailing vessels

Vintage clothing and costumes

Civil War battle sites

Art deco architecture and neon displays

Living history museums

Antique collections and collectibles

Shaker furniture

Victorian crafts

Photography is also an essential element of many history-related fields. Photographers are often employed by archeologists, restoration architects, and museum collection managers.

The photographic possibilities are endless, limited only by your imagination.

How to Market Your Work

Photographers with darkroom facilities or access to a good lab can have their own postcards, posters, and calendars printed and duplicated for minimal costs. Approaching bookstores and gift shops in the region your work covers can result in consignment arrangements or outright sales.

Distributors become necessary for projects with more national appeal. *The Literary Marketplace,* a volume readily available at any library, lists the different distributors and the products they handle.

Greeting card companies are always on the lookout for interesting art. *Writer's Market,* an annual directory of publishers, lists greeting card producers and explains how to approach them.

Proposing a Coffeetable Book

A coffeetable book with color photographs is a much more expensive undertaking, and definitely outside the personal budget of most photographers and writers. Proposing your idea to a publisher is the only way to go.

Michael Larsen, in addition to his *Painted Ladies* series, is the author of the definitive book on the subject of book proposals. Appropriately titled *How to Write a Book Proposal,* it covers everything you need to know to create a successful proposal, including nine criteria for judging your idea, eight things editors look for, and how to submit illustrations. The guide is published by Writers Digest Books.

However, even with the most carefully crafted proposal, you must likely will run into resistance. Many publishers shy away from such projects because of the cost involved.

Michael Larsen and Elizabeth Pomada, even as established literary agents, had difficulty at first convincing a publisher to take on their *Painted Ladies* project. Some were put off because of the cost; others felt that their first book, which covered only San Francisco, was too regional in scope and wouldn't sell enough copies to make it profitable. They were wrong.

An editor from Dutton made a trip to San Francisco and was immediately captivated by the idea. Six books later, and with hundreds of thousands of copies in print, the *Painted Ladies* series started and continues the movement in Victorian restoration.

If your idea is a good one, the quality of your work is exceptional, and you don't give up easily (it took Michael and Elizabeth a year and a half to find their enthusiastic editor), approaching a publisher can eventually pay off.

Further Reading

America's Painted Ladies: The Ultimate Celebration of our Victorians, by Michael Larsen and Elizabeth Pomada. Photographs by Douglas Keister, Dutton-Studio Books.

Domestic Technology: A Chronology of Developments, G. K. Hall. A standard reference for historical writers.

Historic Preservation through Victorian Crafts: A Portrait of Artistic License, by Michael Larsen and Elizabeth Pomada, Dutton-Studio.

How to Write a Book Proposal, by Michael Larsen, Writers Digest Books.

The Literary Marketplace, R. R. Bowker.

Photographer's Market Place, Writers Digest Books.

Writer's Market, Writers Digest Books.

CHAPTER NINE

The Self-Employed History Buff

Profiting from the Past

B usiness-minded history buffs who want to be their own boss and pursue their love of history have successfully ventured into a variety of endeavors. In doing so, they've established businesses satisfying not only their own interests, but also fulfilling the needs of other history buffs. In this chapter you will meet a horse-drawn carriage tour operator in Charleston, South Carolina; an antique and collectibles dealer in Ithaca, New York; an auctioneer from Athens, Pennsylvania; a vintage clothing expert in Fort Lauderdale, Florida; and a historic inn proprietor on Nantucket Island.

Carriage Tour Operator

"There's nothing better than a good mule, there's nothing worse than a bad one," says Tom Doyle, owner of the Palmetto Carriage Works, a horse- and mule-drawn carriage tour company in Charleston, South Carolina. "The thing about the bad ones, though, is that they don't hide it very well. I can spend an afternoon with a mule and know whether or not it's going to work. A horse will go by something 99 times as if it wasn't there, but on the hundredth time, the time you're not paying attention, the horse will absolutely freak out. Mules are much easier to train."

And if anyone should know the characteristics of mules, it's Tom Doyle. He has built up his tour business and now employs 28 people, owns a stable right in the heart of the city, and has 26 carriages, 2 horses, and 28 mules.

"The fellow who began the business started off with just the frame of an old farm wagon," Tom recalls. "He built some seats and a roof on top of it. He also had a carriage from the Jack Daniels Brewery and he picked up a few old carriages from auctions. But they're not really built heavy-duty enough for the kind of work we use them for and they're too small. It's hard to find an antique carriage that will carry 6 or 16 people. Because of that, we began designing our own carriages."

Tom employs one person who does nothing but build carriages. He also has a full barn staff, an office manager, a bookkeeper, a secretary, a ticket collector, and drivers who also double as grooms. But everyone is also a licensed tour guide.

"The key to doing well in the carriage business," Tom explains, "is when the business is here, you've got to be able to handle it, and when it's not here, you have to be able to get real small. We're very seasonal."

Tom Doyle came to Charleston from Massachusetts to study at the Citadel. When he finished with his B.A. in history, he looked around for work he would enjoy. But most of the things he liked to do didn't pay enough money to support a family, so he was often forced to hold down two jobs. Out of this moonlighting, he discovered the Palmetto Carriage Works and started there as a part-time carriage driver–cum–tour guide. Within a year, however, he had graduated to full-time status and was working 60 to 70 hours a week. When the original owner decided it was time to retire in 1982, he offered the business to Tom.

"I didn't have a dime at the time," Tom admits, "but he gave me such a good deal, I was able to go out and find some other people who were willing to invest, and I put together a little group of silent partners."

But it's possible to start small in this business, Tom maintains. You don't need an office or a ticket collector or a fleet of carriages. With an investment of about $6,000—for the carriage, the tack, the animal and various permits—you can position yourself in a place that's visible to tourists, perhaps outside a visitor's information center or near a popular place to stay or visit.

"It's a see-and-do thing," says Tom. "The carriages themselves are the best advertising. Tourists will ask the driver, 'Hey, how do I get on one of these?'" The real bread and butter of the business is the walk-up tourist.

But to make it work you have to live the business, Tom warns. You have to be out there driving every day, making friends and getting to know everyone. Then word of mouth will get you going.

Tom also markets his business to the big hotels in town and the meeting planners and has found his niche with large groups. "People come into town for a conference or some other event, and they might want to do an off-premises function, maybe have dinner at an historic building. I tell them, 'Well, here's what we'll do. We'll pick you up in carriages and transport you there.'"

Tom also runs a free shuttle service with his 1934 antique Ford bus. He moves his customers from the Visitor's Center to his starting point.

Tom's tours are an hour long and cover 20 blocks of the old city. Drivers provide a nonstop narration about Charleston's history, architecture, gardens, people, and points of interest.

"As opposed to a motorized tour, our drivers can turn and talk to the people and make eye contact," Tom says. "It's a leisurely business. While you're waiting for the carriage to fill up, you chat with the passengers. To have a really great tour, you need to get to know your customers. And tourists are great to deal with, because 99.9 percent of them are in a good mood. They're on vacation, after all! When I take people on a carriage tour, everyone in the city benefits, because I leave them so happy with Charleston, they're wanting to do more and to come back."

To have a successful business, you must love the city where you're set up, and you have to be an expert and know everything about its local history. "Good business sense is also important," Tom says, "and when you're the boss you have to monitor your drivers—the tour they give is the most important part. I occasionally pay strangers to ride and check out the drivers."

Tom is convinced that it's more than a job, it's a life-style. "You get to work with the animals, which I really like, you can bring your children to work, and all the neighborhood kids come around the stables to help out and get free rides. You have to do a good job, You're not only representing yourself, you're representing the whole city."

If you can find an Amish settlement, you'll be able to find carriages and farm wagons for sale. There are large settlements in Pennsylvania, Indiana, Ohio, and Tennessee. To help locate these settlements, write or call the state's department of tourism and they'll be able to direct you.

Antique Dealer

"If you scratch a dealer, you'll find a collector underneath," reveals Adam Perl, proprietor of Pastimes, an antiques and collectibles shop in Ithaca, New York. "Many of us have gone into business just to finance our collecting habits." Adam's own collecting habit began in the seventh grade when a classmate brought a book to school called *Cash for Your Coins*. But even if that hadn't happened, it's unlikely the collecting bug would have passed Adam by. He grew up surrounded by art and antiques; his mother is an art historian who worked at the Museum of Modern Art in New York, the Andrew Dickson White Museum at Cornell, and at the Smithsonian's Hirshhorn Museum. His father was a writer, and both parents were serious antique collectors.

Surprisingly, Adam had never been to an auction until he was a young adult. He had just rented an unfurnished apartment when he found out about a country auction being held nearby.

"I was instantly hooked. I spent $100 and filled my van three times. I furnished my entire apartment, with items left over to spare. The early seventies was a golden age of buying, when wonderful three- and four-generation estates were being broken up all over the country, but especially in the Northeast. There wasn't much of an antique market in any field then—you could buy anything for the proverbial song in those days."

With no thought of turning it into a business at that time, Adam began frequenting auctions for the fun of it. He'd go out with $5 or $10 in his pocket and come home with treasures. "I kept doing it over and over again, until I felt I had much more than I could fit in my apartment," he recalls. "I realized from seeing people's setups at flea markets that they had an organized system of pricing and that they generally specialized in a particular area, such as knives or dolls. I learned that if I took the things I bought and cleaned them up a bit—polished the brass, refinished the wood, and stove-blacked the iron—that I could actually sell them for more than I had paid for them. I had my first garage sale and made a little money on it. It wasn't much of a step from that to connect up with New York City and the contacts I had there."

He talked to several dealers and tried to feel out people who were sympathetic and who would teach him. "At the time the world of antiques was pretty much a mystery; there was this arcane underground where people wouldn't reveal their secrets or knowledge to anyone," Adam says.

Adam found his sympathetic antique dealers at American Hurrah, which is now a well-known shop run by Joel and Kate Kopp, specializing in quilts and photographic images. "The Kopps were very forthcoming and didn't hold anything back," he recalls. "They taught me you try to double your money. You don't always do it, or sometimes you do better, but that's what you aim for. They taught me how to judge the condition of an item, and how to develop and trust your own taste. They also helped to bail me out when I made mistakes.

"I became a 'picker,' a term in the industry for a wholesaler. The picker, during his antique hunting expeditions, tries to pick out the 1 great item out of the 10,000 he sees. I would actually buy retail at shops in upstate New York, perhaps finding a quilt, beautifully made and in excellent condition, for $25 to $50. I would take them to the city and sell them for double.

"The Kopps had taught me to look for the fine cotton quilts that were hand-stitched with good colors and good patterns and early nineteenth-century materials. I had bought a quilt at a garage sale for $4 but it didn't meet any of that criteria. It was thick, heavy wool, twentieth-century, rather ugly. But still, there was something about it that was really striking. It had a man's wool tanktop bathing suit stitched into it, complete with its Sears Roebuck label. I took this to New York, but the Kopps didn't think much of it. But they were always very nice to me; they bought the quilt for $12 and I was relieved. Later they turned around and were able to sell it for $50. This quilt was sold many times and eventually ended up in the Louvre Museum in Paris, as an important example of early twentieth-century American folk art. Anybody who's been in business has made mistakes from time to time. Incidents like this can happen to the best of us."

Starting on a Shoestring

Adam opened his first shop in 1973 with just $400. A condemned high school had just been bought by an architect who remodeled it and converted it into a lively arcade of shops and boutiques called the DeWitt Building. Adam rented an unpretentious hole-in-the-wall for $125 a month plus one month's rent as a security deposit. The landlord gave him some paint, and he bought a huge old machine-made oriental rug for $1. "The rug had several feet missing in the corner. I spent another $1 and bought a big overstuffed chair to cover the hole. After the $2 I spent on decor, I had $148 left for merchandise," he says.

Adam left the business for a few years, then returned in 1978 to open his current shop, Pastimes. "This is one of the best businesses to get into on little or no capital," he says. "You don't need any particular expertise, or any particular degree. You do need to have some stock and a couple of tables and table coverings. And then you can hit the flea markets. You can still find perfectly good flea markets where you can set up for $10 to $25. Later you can graduate to a little bit higher-caliber show, whose fees might be from $35 to $100. A lot of people just do shows. It's the exception actually having a retail shop. You're tied down and have the overhead.

"Many people get started in this business as they're heading toward retirement. They ease into it the last 5 or 10 years of their working career, and then do it as a retirement business to supplement their pensions and social security income.

"And, it's a recession-resistent business. When times are hard, antiques are a better buy than new items. People are shopping more carefully, and even noncollectors who just want to get good practical furniture, tools, or gifts will turn to antiques."

Adam is a firm believer that in this business, the less money you have, the better. "I knew a young man who had inherited $50,000. This was many years ago when that was really a lot of money. He went out and bought every exquisite piece of furniture he could find. I remember at the auctions I was very jealous; he could outbid everybody. He opened up a shop with all those beautiful things, but he couldn't sell them because he'd paid too much for them. You have to develop through experience knowledge of what the market will bear. There's no substitute for the actual buying and selling of merchandise to learn about the market and pricing. There are thousands of antique price guides, but this is something you can't really learn by the book. It's best to get into it gradually, go to a lot of antique shows and shops, compare prices, do your homework."

And you have to be careful about where you buy your merchandise, Adam warns. It's vital to make sure the auctioneers and dealers are reputable. "There's a great deal of dishonesty in the business," Adam admits. "A dealer might misrepresent an item's condition or authenticity. It's easy to get caught. Fairly recently a local dealer of questionable repute came across a big stash of mint-condition German lithographs that were reported to be from the turn of the century. We'd never seen anything like it—there are certain processes you just can't duplicate, and this was one of them. The dealers were scarfing them up for $7 to $10 apiece. We found out they were repros, but not before a lot of us got stung.

"And 10 years ago I was selling some red-colored Fiestaware, a very popular deco dinnerware made by Homer Laughlin in the thirties, forties, and fifties. It turned out to be radioactive. Some of the glazes had been made with uranium."

Choose Your Specialty

There are probably more than 10,000 branches in the antiques and collectibles business. Some collectors specialize in nothing but actual items used in the Civil War. You can take any particular area of your interest, whether it be local history, silver making, the history of advertising, woodworking, tools, lace making, or photographica, and turn that one area into a whole specialty and a whole business.

"Look for an area you love," Adam advises, "and learn more about it and concentrate in it. I specialize in about five or six areas I happen to have a particular love and feeling for—antique buttons, costume jewelry from the Victorian era through the forties, 1910 postcards, fountain pens, sterling silver, and antique beads. We also carry some oak furniture, glassware, and pho-tographica. Pastimes is relatively small, but it looks like a well-organized and cleaned-up flea market."

Adam loves what he's doing, always chasing after the next bargain, enjoying the wonderful thrill of the hunt, that feeling you get looking for treasures and bargains. "It keeps you excited and fueled up when you're unloading your van in the cold rain, or you're stuck in the mud at an auction."

Auctioneer

"I have this nice oak rolltop desk, how about a five hundred dollar bid, get five hundred, get five hundred, get two and a half, start us off, give us a hundred, give a hundred . . ." is part of the chant you'll hear from auctioneer Jim Ridolfi, owner of the Aspon Trading Company in Troy, Pennsylvania. "Everyone has a chant, and everyone develops their own," Jim says. "I try not to use too many words—the people won't understand you. What they're listening for is the numbers. You learn a basic method at auctioneer training school, and then you take it and refine it and make it into your own."

Background

Training programs can run from two weeks to three or four months, depending on your state's requirements. While in training, auctioneers also study communications skills; the law as applied to auctioneers; marketing and advertising; auction management; appraisal; and selling real estate.

Different states have different licensing laws: some states have none at all, some are very rigorous with what they require.

Many auctioneers go through various national auctioneering schools; the best-known one is the Missouri Auction School. But it's important to check first which schools your state will accept. Pennsylvania, for example, only accepts training through the two schools in Pennsylvania. The best thing to do is contact your state licensing board and find out what it requires, then write or call the National Auctioneers Association (listed in Appendix C) to find the appropriate training.

Like Jim Ridolfi, many auctioneers are also antique dealers. Jim specializes in old phonographs and radios and has a particular love for mid- to late-nineteenth-century items. In addition to antiques, auctioneers also handle household items, livestock, and real estate.

Jim became an auctioneer in 1992. He advertises his services in newspapers and has made contacts with other antique dealers, estate attorneys, and will executors.

Auctioneers hold their events indoors in hotel ballrooms or outside in a farmer's field or an estate's backyard. They work on a percentage basis, earning between 15 and 30 percent of the price of each item sold.

In addition to the auctioneer, there are other employment possibilities working in and around auctions:

Runners move the items for sale from the holding area to the state.

Floor Managers supervise the runners, let them know which items are going up next, and take care of any other details so that the auctioneer is not distracted.

Clerks make a record of the proceedings and handle the numbering of lots and bidders.

Cashiers collect the money.

Security Guards watch over the sold items while they're waiting to be picked up.

Caterers provide the refreshments for the audience and staff.

Advertisers and Marketers help the auctioneer inform the public about his or her services and particular auction events.

Catalogers work with large estates, organizing the items and taking precise inventories.

Appraisers help authenticate and place a value on particular items.

Furniture Refinishers and Restorers, while not usually working directly with an auction, find work with dealers or private individuals giving life back to old or damaged items.

Flea Market and Antique Show Organizers put on the big events that attract thousands of people. They handle every detail, including advertising, allocating space, and collecting fees.

Vintage Clothing Specialist

Most children love to play dress-up, and Mary Ptak, co-owner of the Stock Exchange, a vintage clothing shop in Fort Lauderdale, Florida, was no exception. "I wanted to spend all my time in people's attics," Mary confesses. "I was mainly interested in finding old-style clothing. When I was in college in the sixties, I would just literally knock on strangers' doors and ask them if I could clean out their attics. In those days, they were usually delighted for you to do that."

But times have changed, and people are much more aware of the treasures they might have stored away. "Gone are the days when you could pick up something for 25 cents or under," Mary says.

Mary and her partner, Carol Levin, have been in business since 1986. They were both dissatisfied with their jobs, and one day they just decided to take the plunge. Carol loves the sales end of the business, dealing with the customers, and Mary satisfies her shopping urges by traveling around the country as the Stock Exchange's buyer.

Over the years they've managed to build up an international clientele, including collectors from Japan, Germany, and England. "Our customers are an eclectic mix of people," Mary says. "People from England and Japan have been buying up everything they can find from the fifties. Our serious collectors tend to buy clothes from the thirties through the fifties—Joan Crawford, Great Gatsby and Garbo styles with big padded shoulders and lots of sparkly glitz. Lilli Ann suits from the forties and fifties are popular now, too. They're extremely classy looking, nipped in at the waist with flaring peplums. Some of our customers are Victorian period collectors; but most people now want the article they're buying to be useful—they want to be able to wear it.

"Local kids are demanding sixties and seventies garments. The kids even want the polyester nik-nik shirts from the sixties—foul-looking things, but they're popular now. The kids are always a little more savvy than the general public, and they start fashion trends with their regular street clothes. I used to be able to buy what I liked; now I have to think in terms of my customers' needs."

The Stock Exchange carries clothes ranging in price from $5 for an Indian cotton gauze blouse from the 1960s to a $2,000 Schaparelli gown. Mary and Carol also handle rentals, outfit murder mystery events, and have supplied the costumes for several major television shows and motion pictures, including "Key West," *Cape Fear*, and *Wrestling Ernest Hemingway*.

Mary travels all over the country to look for just the right pieces. She also has built up a network of people who ship her good finds.

"I learned what was collectible from being in the business a long time," Mary explains. "You have to have a good eye to pick what people want and you have to change with the times—trends are constantly changing, and you can't always be buying the same things."

For anyone considering a similar business, Mary cautions that it is important to buy clothes that are in excellent condition, unless it's something that's really ancient and people would expect to be damaged. "And you also need a huge amount of stock. When we started out we had very little, but we took consignments then, and because I'm a fanatic shopper, it didn't take long to build it up."

They've also managed to build themselves a first-class reputation. "We make an effort to pay people what they deserve for their merchandise—it's one of the reasons we've been so successful," Mary says.

The Stock Exchange is a classic example of laughing all the way to the bank. In 1986 no one would give them a business loan. "They didn't think we'd make it," Mary says with just a tad of righteous indignation in her voice.

The two partners are currently opening another store in a popular area in Fort Lauderdale. *Jezebel*, as they've called it, will carry upscale vintage clothing, accessories, and antiques.

Mary is kept very busy getting ready for the opening. The one think she doesn't have time to do anymore is hunt through people's attics. These days she can hire other people to do that.

Historic Inn Proprietor

Many entrepreneurial history buffs have been caught up in a popular movement throughout the country—restoring and refurbishing historic homes and converting them into country inns, guest houses, and bed and breakfast establishments. Nantucket, Massachusetts, is filled with such historic homes, including an inn owned by Roger and Mary Schmidt.

A Bit of History

The name *Nantucket* is an American Indian word meaning "faraway land," and though this crescent-shaped island is only 30 miles off the coast of Massachusetts, it is, indeed, set apart with an Old World flavor all its own. Ferries transport visitors and residents back and forth between the island and the town of Hyannis on Cape Cod. Stepping off that ferry is like taking a step back in time to an age gone by.

Settled in 1659 (the Nine Original Purchasers, as they were called, gained possession from the English for the sum of 30 pounds and 2 beaver hats), the island prospered well into the mid-1800s as a major whaling port. But the invention of kerosene, an encroaching sandbar blocking the harbor, and the lure of the California Gold Rush all contributed to a quick demise. Not too much later, Americans began the now deeply ingrained tradition of summer vacations, and Nantucket was rediscovered. Business-minded homemakers turned their stately houses into guest inns or restaurants, and a new breed of fisher emerged to supply the "summer people" with Nantucket's bounty of shellfish: littleneck and cherrystone clams, quahogs, mussels, and the famous, succulent bay scallops.

Today tourism still supports the 7,000 or so year-round residents (the summer population blossoms to near 40,000 each year), but the character of the island hasn't changed much over the years. Though pleasure boats have replaced the old wooden whaling vessels, the original Quaker homes, simple but sturdy dwellings, and the perfectly preserved Georgian, Federal, and Greek Revival-style houses still stand in orderly ranks along cobblestoned Main Street and the other winding lanes and crisscrossing pathways of Nantucket Town.

Stroll down any narrow byway and take a peek into postage-stamp gardens filled with flowering rhododendron, azaleas, and other perennials. Some of the houses are impressive mansions, the legacy of the wealth-producing whaling industry. Others are small dollhouses with geranium-filled planter boxes sitting below lacy-curtained, leaded-glass windows.

A glimpse inside any of the homes reveals Old World mahogany antiques—carved sea chests and canopied or sleigh-back beds—many with shiny brass or even solid silver fixtures. White wicker rockers grace wooden porches, and widow's walks curve around under cedar-shake roof shingles.

The Nantucket Historical Association has a strong influence, and strict building codes are enthusiastically adhered to by residents. Though other tourist spots are often marred by lines of fast-food stands and high-rise hotels, no intrusive golden arches or glaring neon signs are allowed on the island. Even the gas stations are disguised, their red brick structures blending perfectly with their surroundings. So esthetically pleasing is the island that American architects repeatedly vote Nantucket as the only "perfect 10" in the country.

Architecture and history buffs have, for a start, the Old Mill, the Jethro Coffin House, considered the oldest house on the island, and the Whaling Museum to discover, as well as all the other designated landmarks. In fact, the entire town of Nantucket has been included as a district on the National Register of Historic Places.

Many of Nantucket's historic homes are now open to the public as museums, and others have become established as quaint and comfortable guest houses and inns.

The Inn at 18 Gardner Street

Roger and Mary Schmidt's inn is called simply the 18 Gardner Street Inn, on Nantucket Island. The colonial-style house, which is on the historical walking tour, was originally built in 1835 by Captain Robert Joy. The sea captain took the proceeds of his last whaling excursion and built the house to retire in. Over the years the home was owned by several different families. In the 1940s the property was converted to a lodging house with six or seven rooms. The next family that purchased the inn installed bathrooms in the rooms and ran it as a bed and breakfast.

The Schmidts acquired the inn in 1988. The building is a traditional square box shape with a pitched roof and an ell in the back where the kitchen was added in the late 1800s. In front there's a center door with original hand-rolled glass windows on each side. A typical Nantucket friendship staircase graces the front door, with steps on either side meeting at the landing at the top. Weathered cedar shakes (which, along with the famous Nantucket fog, help to contribute to the island's other nickname, the Grey Lady) and a large widow's walk complete the picture of an elegant sea captain's mansion.

Spread through the inn's two stories and finished third-floor attic are 12 guestrooms furnished with pencil-post, canopied, and four-poster beds, and antique mahogany or cherry dressers and nightstands. All of the rooms are airy; many are spacious suites, most with working fireplaces.

Roger and Mary and their two children occupy a two-bedroom apartment in the finished basement. During the first two years they owned the inn, the Schmidts completely refurnished it. In the third and fourth years they started doing massive restoration to the guest rooms. They took all the wallpaper down and repaired the dozens of cracks they discovered in the plaster. They upgraded the bathrooms and, keeping the period appearance to the bedrooms, rewallpapered with pastels and satin wall coverings. They completely gutted the kitchen and replaced it with a new commercial kitchen so they could serve guests a full breakfast. And, as so often happens in old houses, they discovered a beautiful fireplace hidden for years behind one of the plaster walls. Every three years or so, the exterior of the house gets a new paint job.

One thing the Schmidts avoided was putting up new walls. They specifically chose an inn that wouldn't require massive reconstruction work. From experience they learned that putting up sheet rock can get unbelievably expensive and complicated, dealing with commercial building codes. Because their property had been licensed for so many years as an inn, they didn't have to be relicensed, although they do have to get an annual license through the local building inspector.

Background

The Schmidts are originally from Springfield, in western Massachusetts. They honeymooned on Nantucket in 1977 and fell in love with the island. They started coming three and four times a year. But when they started hunting for property to buy, it soon became obvious that the selling prices were way out of their reach.

Roger explains:

In the early eighties, property on Nantucket skyrocketed. I was in the electronics field, Mary worked in a photography lab, and the dream of owning a summer home got pushed aside because of economics. We went to the nearby island of Martha's Vineyard because we'd heard there were good buys there. We ended up finding some property there and got into the real estate business. We bought a mariner's home and completely restored it and turned it into a small, five-bedroom inn, and developed some other pieces of property there as well. This was all happening while we were still considering Springfield as our main residence. Eventually we sold it all off and came back to Nantucket in a much better financial condition to buy our current property.

We had an innkeeper running 18 Gardner Street for us for two years, but we almost went bankrupt because of mismanagement. So in April of 1990 we moved to the island permanently and took over running the inn. Business then took off like a cannonball. As terrible as this may sound, anybody who gets into this business and thinks they will succeed by serving the greatest cup of coffee and greeting every guest with a warm smile, is totally wrong. It's not enough. You have to sell your property to a person on the other end of the phone. Unfortunately, for that person, he doesn't know what he's getting. He can't see it and touch it. So through written advertisements in major newspapers such as the *Boston Globe* and the *New York Times*, and through verbal communications, you have to get across to your potential guests what your facilities are. Then when they come, you can give them the greatest cup of coffee and the warmest smile.

But that's still not enough. You have to understand your guests' needs and try to meet them. For example, we listened to our guests and learned that it was an inconvenience for them to have to walk downtown to pick up their rented bicycles. So we bought bicycles and provide them to our guests free of charge. We also learned that in the autumn, it could be a long, cold walk back from town, so that's when we made sure all our fireplaces were working. That keeps the fall business coming in. Again, we listened and learned that guests would like a little more than a muffin and coffee for breakfast, so we got a food service permit and offer a full meal in the morning. We also provide dockside shuttle service from the ferry to the inn, picnic baskets, beach blankets, and ice coolers. We do what we can to make our guests happy. This has helped to substantially build up our word-of-mouth referral business.

A lot of people want to live out their romantic dream by retiring to an idyllic spot such as Nantucket and running a bed and breakfast. But the first major mistake they make is when they use the word "retiring." There's nothing retiring, or romantic, about operating an inn. You have to work very hard.

From April 1 to November 31, my day is primarily involved with taking reservations and handling problems and delegating responsibilities to our staff of five. During the winter, we involve ourselves with marketing and interior design and restoration. We're always busy."

Financial Considerations

Roger Schmidt has learned over the years how to handle the financial aspects of inn proprietorship. He says:

In 1988, we paid $850,000 for our historic inn, and at the time, that was a good price. The property dropped in value to $600,000 in the next two years, but now because of the restoration and the steady clientele we've built up, our property, and our business, is worth slightly over $1 million.

Right now our rooms are full about 100 days of the year, and we are aiming to have full occupancy every weekend through the off-season months. The inn is an upscale one, and our high season rates are from $140 to $170 a night. But our monthly operating expenses and our mortgage payments are very high, too.

Nantucket, of course, is a small and very expensive island. There are many areas in the country where you could pick up a small house or an established inn for around $100,000.

Whatever the value, the trick is to have an understanding of real estate financing and to try to be a little creative. In our case, we put very little down; the owner was willing to hold back a second mortgage. Another alternative is to lease with an option to buy. We've just done that with the property adjoining ours, and now we have five more guest rooms to book.

But I would advise starting out with a property with just three or four guest rooms. It's a very risky business and there's a high burnout and turnover rate. Sometimes the dream can turn into a nightmare.

You can't treat it as a dream. You have to treat it as a business.

Further Information

Magazines can help the self-employed history buff feel connected in the field. Try *Antique Trader*, *Maine Antique Digest*, or *Newtown Bee*. You might also look for the following books:

How to Start and Run a Bed & Breakfast Inn by Ripley Hotch and Carl Glassman, Stackpole Books. Covers buying the right inn, attracting guests, estimating costs and profitability.

The Seventh Old House Catalog, by Lawrence Grow, Sterling/Main Street Publishing. An A-to-Z sourcebook for restoration and remodeling.

Sotheby's Caring for Antiques, edited by Mette Tang Simpson and Michael Huntley, Simon & Schuster. A guide to handling, cleaning, displaying, and restoring antiques.

CHAPTER TEN

Other Jobs for History Buffs

Here are a few other employment possibilities not covered in previous chapters.

Education

Teachers must have a special talent; they carry a weighty responsibility. How they present their subject will affect their students' attitudes toward history for a lifetime. A good teacher will know how to make history come alive and can show its importance to our lives today and for our future.

History courses are generally taught all throughout elementary, middle, and secondary schools. A teacher would need at least a bachelor's degree in history or history education.

To teach at the college level, a master's degree would be required—and in many cases, a doctorate. At the graduate level, teachers would need to specialize in a particular area such as American civilization or European history.

Educators also work in museums, presenting programs to the public and participating on curatorial teams to make sure the information being presented in exhibits is easily accessible to the audience.

Some private organizations, such as Crow Canyon Archaeological Center, also employ educators to provide orientation information and training to participants.

Educators can find work with historical societies or preservation boards as information officers or in public relations.

The "Ologies"

Anthropology

Anthropology, the study of human beings, has four subdivisions: archeology (which was discussed in Chapter 7), cultural anthropology, physical anthropology, and linguistics.

Cultural anthropology looks at all of the manifestations of culture, including early civilizations that are now extinct, up through current groups of people that exist today. Ethnology is a branch of cultural anthropology that looks at the historical development of cultures, the distinguishing characteristics of the different races, and the similarities and differences between cultures.

Physical anthropology studies early people and evolution. Linguistics is the science of language and how it develops. The field of linguistics is further divided into historical, descriptive, and applied linguistics.

Anthropologists work in academic settings or live in the field among different groups and indigenous cultures.

Paleontology

Paleontologists are concerned with the forms of life existing in earlier periods. They study fossilized plants, animals, and bones and find work in academic settings or with natural history museums.

Geology

Geology is the science that deals with the physical history of the earth. Geologists study rocks and the physical changes the earth has undergone. In addition to teaching, geologists work for engineering firms, oil companies, and with architects and archeologists.

Living History Museums

Burroughs Home
2505 First Street
Fort Myers, FL
(813) 332-1229

Hancock Shaker Village
Pittsfield, MA
(413) 443-0188

Colonial Williamsburg
Employment Office
P.O. Box 1776
Williamsburg, VA 23187
Telephone: (804) 220-7000
Job Line: (804) 220-7129
Visitor Information: (800)228-8878

Kamoklia Hawaiian Folk Village
Kauai, HA
(808) 822-1192

Lowell National Historical Park
Lowell, MA
(508) 459-1000

Oconaluftee Indian Village
Cherokee, NC
(704) 497-2111

Old Salem
Winston-Salem, NC
(919) 721-7300

Old Sturbridge Village
1 Old Sturbridge Village Road
Sturbridge, MA 01566

Plimoth Plantation
P.O. Box 1620
Plymouth, MA 02360
(508) 746-1622

St. Augustine's Spanish Quarter
Historic St. Augustine
  Preservation Board
P.O. Box 1987
St. Augustine, FL 32085
(904) 825-5033

Stuhr Museum of the Prairie
  Pioneer
Grand Island, NE
(308) 381-5316

Westville
Lumpkin, GA
(912) 838-6310

National Park Service Regional Offices

Alaska Region
National Park Service
2525 Gambell Street
Anchorage, AK 99503
(907) 257-2574

Pacific Northwest Region
National Park Service
83 South King Street, #212
Seattle, WA 98104
(206) 553-4409

Western Region
National Park Service
600 Harrison Street, #600
San Francisco, CA 94107
(415) 744-3888

Rocky Mountain Region
National Park Service
P.O. Box 25287
Denver, CO 80225
(303) 969-2777

Southwest Region
National Park Service
P.O. Box 728
Santa Fe, NM 87501
(505) 988-6076

Midwest Region
National Park Service
1709 Jackson Street
Omaha, NE 68102
(402) 221-3456

Southeast Region
National Park Service
Richard B. Russell Federal Bldg.
75 Spring Street, SW
Atlanta, GA 30303
(404) 331-5711

Mid-Atlantic Region
National Park Service
143 South Third Street
Philadelphia, PA 19106
(215) 597-4971

National Capital Region
National Park Service
1100 Ohio Drive, SW
Washington, DC 20242
(202) 619-7256

North Atlantic Region
National Park Service
15 State Street
Boston, MA 02109
(617) 223-5101

Associations

T he following list of associations can be used as a valuable resource guide in locating additional information about specific careers. Many of the organizations publish newsletters listing job and internship opportunities, and still others offer an employment service to members.

ES beneath a listing designates an employment service. NL indicates a newsletter.

Advisory Council on Historic
  Preservation
1100 Pennsylvania Avenue, NW
Washington, DC 20004
(202) 786-0503

American Anthropological
  Association
1703 New Hampshire Avenue,
  NW
Washington, DC 20009
(202) 232-8800

American Association for Museum
  Volunteers
6307 Hardy Drive
McLean, VA 22101
(707) 356-0369
NL

American Association of
  Museums
1225 Eye Street, Suite 200
Washington, DC 20005
(202) 289-1818
NL

American Association for State
  and Local History
172 Second Ave North
Nashville, TN 37201
(615) 255-2971
ES, NL

American Craft Council
Information Center
72 Spring Street
New York, NY 10012
(212) 274-0630

American Historic Association
400 A Street, SE
Washington, DC 20003
(202) 544-2422
ES, NL

American Institute of Architects
1735 New York Ave, NW
Washington, DC 20006
(202) 626-7300
ES, NL

American Library Association
50 E. Huron Street
Chicago, IL 60611
(312) 944-6780
ES, NL

Archaeological Institute of
   America
675 Commonwealth Avenue
Boston, MA 02215
(617) 353-9361
NL

Association for Gravestone Studies
30 Elm Street
Worcester, MA 01609
(508) 831-7753
NL

Association for Living Historical
   Farms and Agricultural Museums
National Museum of American
   History
Room 5035
Smithsonian Institution
Washington, DC 20560
(202) 357-2095
ES

Bureau of the Census
U.S. Department of Commerce
Washington, DC 20233
(301) 763-4040

Costume Society of America
55 Edgewater Drive
P.O. Box 73
Earleville, MD 21919
(410) 275-2329
NL

Genealogical Library
Church of Jesus Christ of
   Latter-day Saints
Family History Library
35 N. West Temple
Salt Lake City, UT 84150
(801) 240-2331

Museum Reference Center
Office of Museum Programs
A&I Building, Room 2235
Smithsonian Institution
Washington, DC 20560
(202) 357-3101

National Archives
Eighth and Constitution
   Avenue
Washington, DC 20408
(202) 501-5402

National Association of
   Government Archives and
   Records Administrators
c/o Director, New York State
   Archives
10A46 Cultural Education
   Center
Albany, NY 12230
(518) 473-8037
NL

National Auctioneers
   Association
8880 Ballentine
Overland, KS 66214
(913) 541-8084
NL

National Center for the Study of
    History
Career Project
Rural Route #1, P.O. Box 679
Cornish, ME 04020

National Conference of SHPOs
Suite 332, Hall of the States
444 North Capitol Street
Washington, DC 20001-1512
(202) 624-5465

National Genealogical Society
4527 Seventeenth Street, N
Arlington, VA 22207-2399
(703) 525-0050
NL

National Register of Historic Places
U.S. Department of the Interior
National Park Service
P.O. Box 37127
Washington, DC 20013-7127
(202) 343-9536

National Trust for Historic
    Preservation
1785 Massachusetts Ave, NW
Washington, DC 20036
(202) 673-4000
ES, NL

Oral History Association
1093 Broxton Avenue, #720
Los Angeles, CA 90024
(213) 825-0597
NL

Organization of American
    Historians
112 N. Bryan Street
Bloomington, IN 47408
(812) 855-7311
ES, NL

Society for American
    Archaeology
808 Seventeenth Street, NW
Suite 200
Washington, DC 20006-3953
(202) 223-9774
ES, NL

Society of American
    Archivists
600 S. Federal, Suite 504
Chicago, IL 60605
(312) 922-0140
NL

Society of Architectural
    Historians
1232 Pine Street
Philadelphia, PA 19107
(215) 735-0224
NL

The Victorian Society in
    America
219 S. Sixth Street
Philadelphia, PA 19106
(215) 627-4252

Further Reading

A Guide to Artifacts of Colonial America, by Ivor Noel Hume, Alfred A. Knopf.
The American Heritage Book of Great Historic Places, American Heritage Publishing Co., Inc.
America Then & Now, edited by David Cohen, Harper San Francisco. Period photographs paired with new ones to show the changes in America.
Peterson's Guide to Graduate and Professional Programs: An Overview, Peterson's Guides, Princeton, N.J.
1001 Things Everyone Should Know about American History, by J. A. Garraty, Doubleday.

The following books can be ordered through the American Association for State and Local History, 172 Second Ave North, Nashville, TN 37201, (615) 255-2971:

A Living History Reader, by Jay Anderson. An anthology of articles written about living history by museum interpreters and enthusiasts.
Directory of American Organizations in the United States and Canada, by the American Association for State and Local History. More than 13,000 listings of historical and genealogical societies, museums, archives, and other history-related groups.
Furniture Care and Conservation, by Robert F. McGiffin. Techniques for museums, dealers, and collectors on methods and products for preserving furniture.
Interpretation of Historic Sites, by William T. Alderson and Shirley Payne Low. How to develop and conduct interpretive programs.
Introduction to Museum Work, by G. Ellis Burcaw. For museum workers worldwide. Covers collections, interpretation, educational programs, exhibits.

Listing of State Historic Preservation Officers (SHPOs), available from the National Conference of SHPOs, Suite 332, Hall of the States, 444 North Capitol St., Washington, D.C., 20001-1512, (202) 624-5465.

National Register of Historic Places, 1966–1988, by the American Association for State and Local History, National Park Service, and National Conference of State Historic Preservation Officers. Listing of more than 50,000 designations by the National Park Service as places worthy of preservation.

Recreating the Historic House Interior, by William Seale. Covers methods for restoration, researching, architectural decisions, floors, wall coverings, and lighting.

Chronicle Guidance Publications puts out a series of briefs explaining the following positions: Anthropologists, Archeologists, Criminologists, Demographers, Economists, Genealogists, Geographers, Librarians, Linguists, Museum Curators, Political Scientists, Sociologists.

They can be ordered through:

Chronicle Guidance Publications
Aurora Street
P.O. Box 1190
Moravia, NY 13118-1190

VGM CAREER BOOKS

CAREER DIRECTORIES
Careers Encyclopedia
Dictionary of Occupational Titles
Occupational Outlook Handbook

CAREERS FOR
Animal Lovers
Bookworms
Caring People
Computer Buffs
Crafty People
Culture Lovers
Environmental Types
Film Buffs
Foreign Language Aficionados
Good Samaritans
Gourmets
History Buffs
Kids at Heart
Nature Lovers
Night Owls
Number Crunchers
Plant Lovers
Shutterbugs
Sports Nuts
Travel Buffs
Writers

CAREERS IN
Accounting; Advertising;
Business; Child Care;
Communications; Computers;
Education; Engineering;
the Environment; Finance;
Government; Health Care; High
Tech; International Business;
Journalism; Law; Marketing;
Medicine; Science; Social &
Rehabilitation Services

CAREER PLANNING
Admissions Guide to Selective
Business Schools
Beating Job Burnout
Beginning Entrepreneur
Career Planning & Development
for College Students & Recent
Graduates
Career Change
Careers Checklists
Complete Guide to Career
Etiquette
Cover Letters They Don't Forget
Dr. Job's Complete Career Guide

Executive Job Search Strategies
Guide to Basic Cover Letter
Writing
Guide to Basic Résumé Writing
Guide to Temporary
Employment
Job Interviewing for College
Students
Joyce Lain Kennedy's Career
Book
Out of Uniform
Slam Dunk Résumés

CAREER PORTRAITS
Animals; Cars; Computers;
Electronics; Fashion;
Firefighting; Music; Nursing;
Sports; Teaching; Travel; Writing

GREAT JOBS FOR
Communications Majors
Engineering Majors
English Majors
Foreign Language Majors
History Majors
Psychology Majors

HOW TO
Approach an Advertising Agency
and Walk Away with the Job
You Want
Bounce Back Quickly After
Losing Your Job
Choose the Right Career
Cómo escribir un currículum
vitae en inglés que tenga éxito
Find Your New Career Upon
Retirement
Get & Keep Your First Job
Get Hired Today
Get into the Right Business
School
Get into the Right Law School
Get People to Do Things Your
Way
Have a Winning Job Interview
Hit the Ground Running in Your
New Job
Hold It All Together When
You've Lost Your Job
Improve Your Study Skills
Jump Start a Stalled Career
Land a Better Job

Launch Your Career in TV News
Make the Right Career Moves
Market Your College Degree
Move from College into a
Secure Job
Negotiate the Raise You Deserve
Prepare a Curriculum Vitae
Prepare for College
Run Your Own Home Business
Succeed in College
Succeed in High School
Take Charge of Your Child's
Early Education
Write a Winning Résumé
Write Successful Cover Letters
Write Term Papers & Reports
Write Your College Application
Essay

MADE EASY
Cover Letters
Job Hunting
Job Interviews
Résumés

OPPORTUNITIES IN
This extensive series provides
detailed information on nearly
150 individual career fields.

RÉSUMÉS FOR
Advertising Careers
Banking and Financial Careers
Business Management Careers
College Students &
Recent Graduates
Communications Careers
Education Careers
Engineering Careers
Environmental Careers
Ex-Military Personnel
50+ Job Hunters
Health and Medical Careers
High School Graduates
High Tech Careers
Law Careers
Midcareer Job Changes
Re-Entering the Job Market
Sales and Marketing Careers
Scientific and Technical Careers
Social Service Careers
The First-Time Job Hunter

VGM Career Horizons
a division of *NTC Publishing Group*
4255 West Touhy Avenue
Lincolnwood, Illinois 60646–1975